Samara Golden

Edited and with an essay by Catherine Craft

NASHER SCULPTURE CENTER
DELMONICO BOOKS • D.A.P., NEW YORK

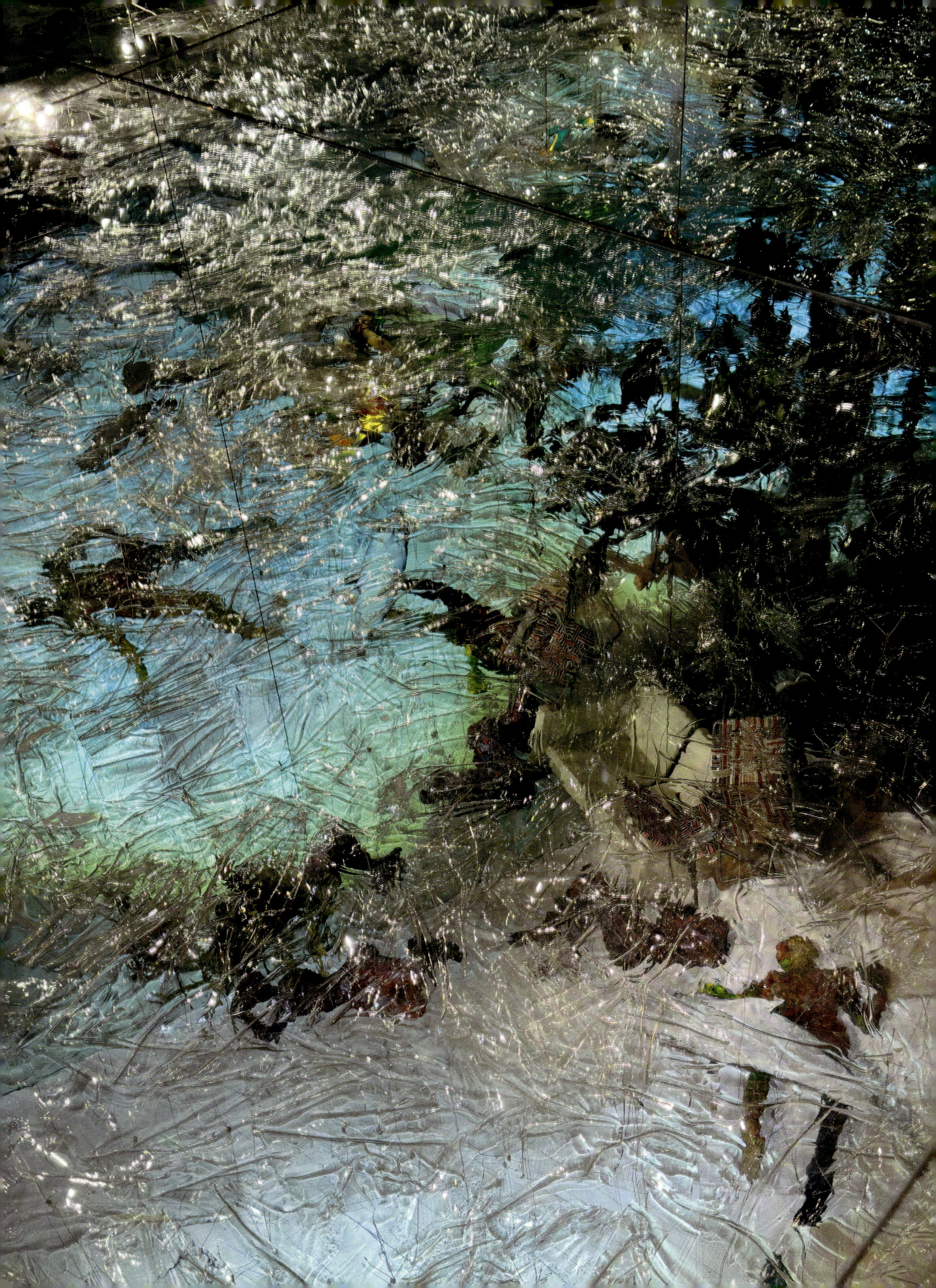

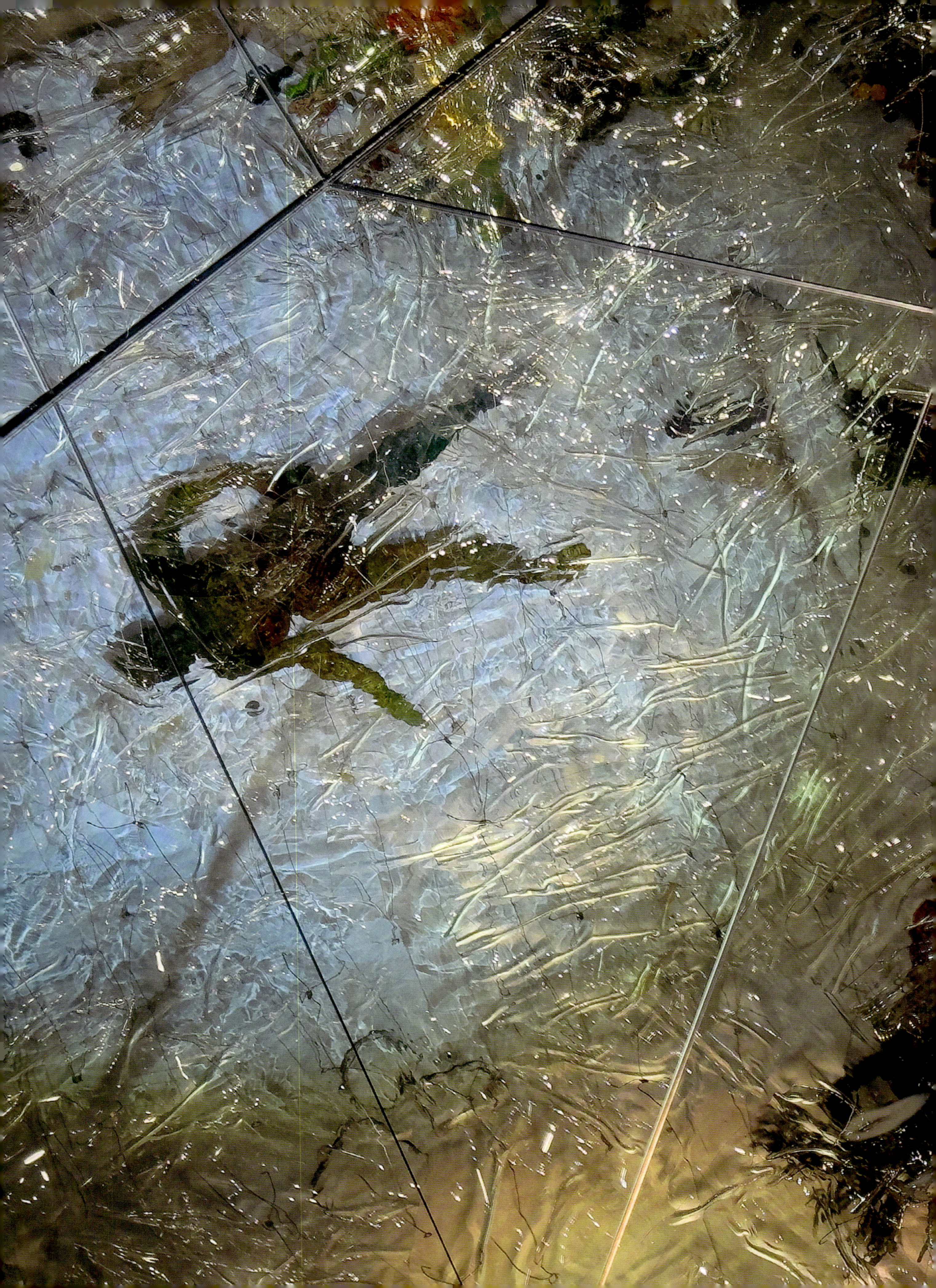

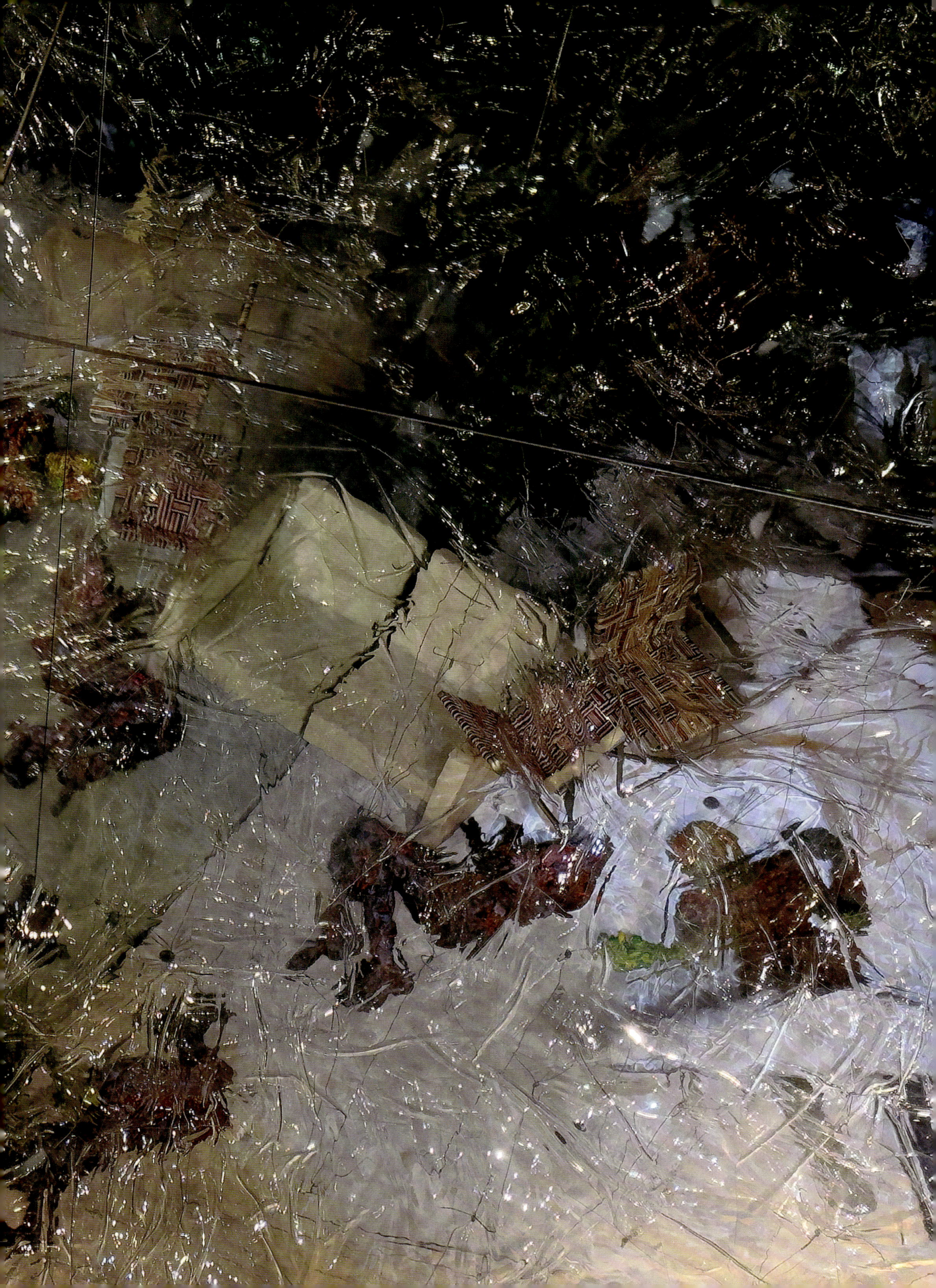

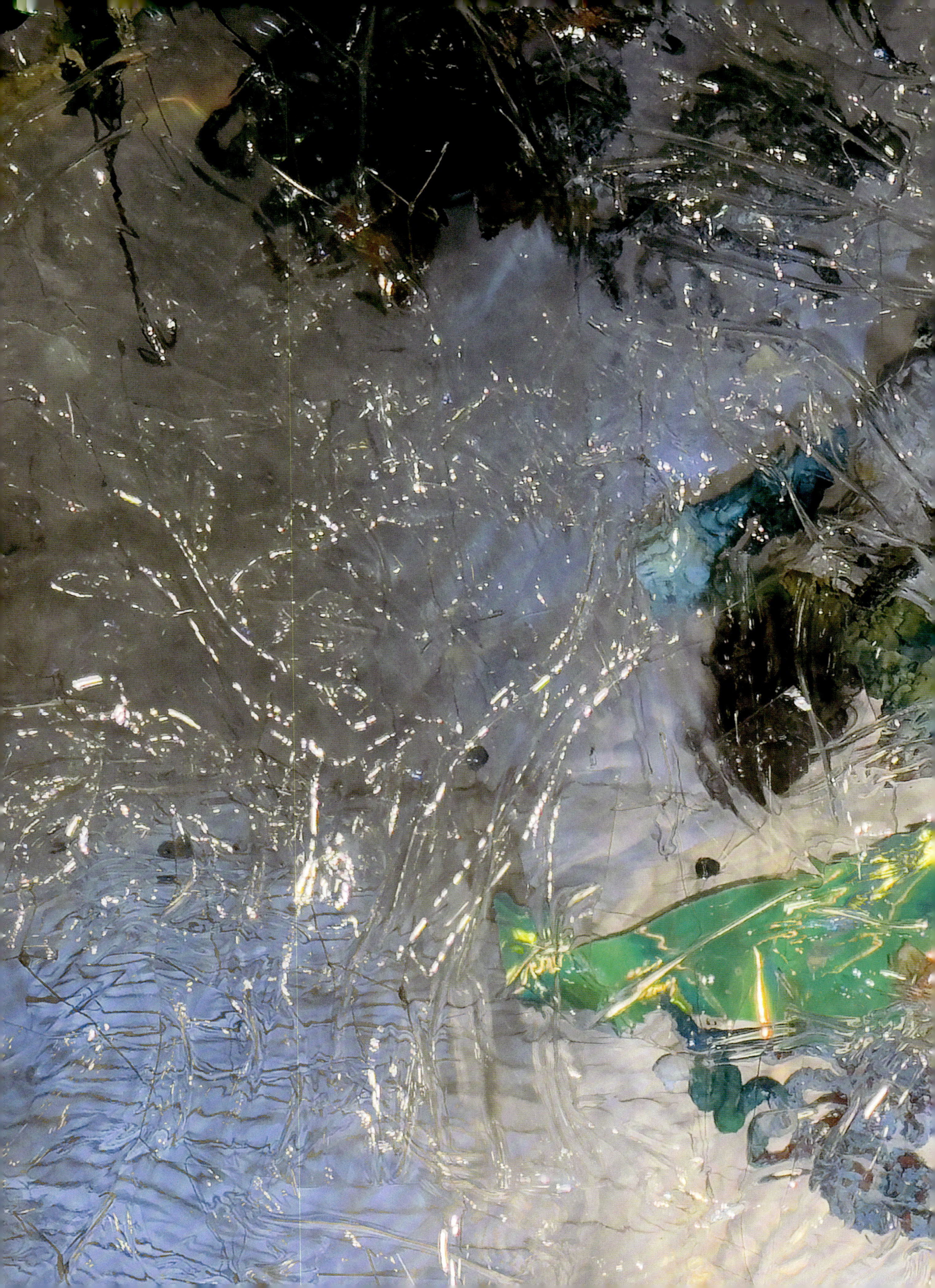

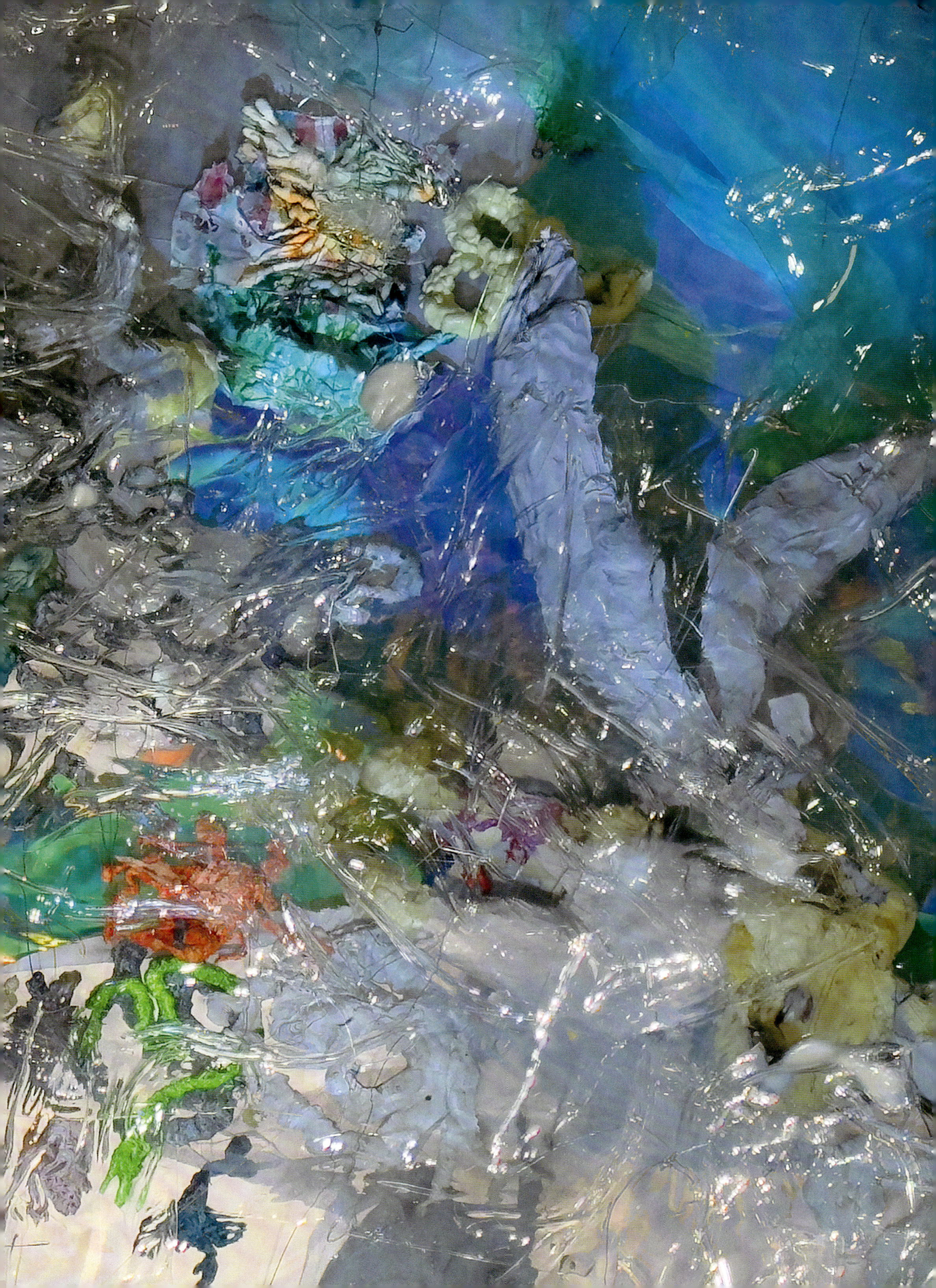

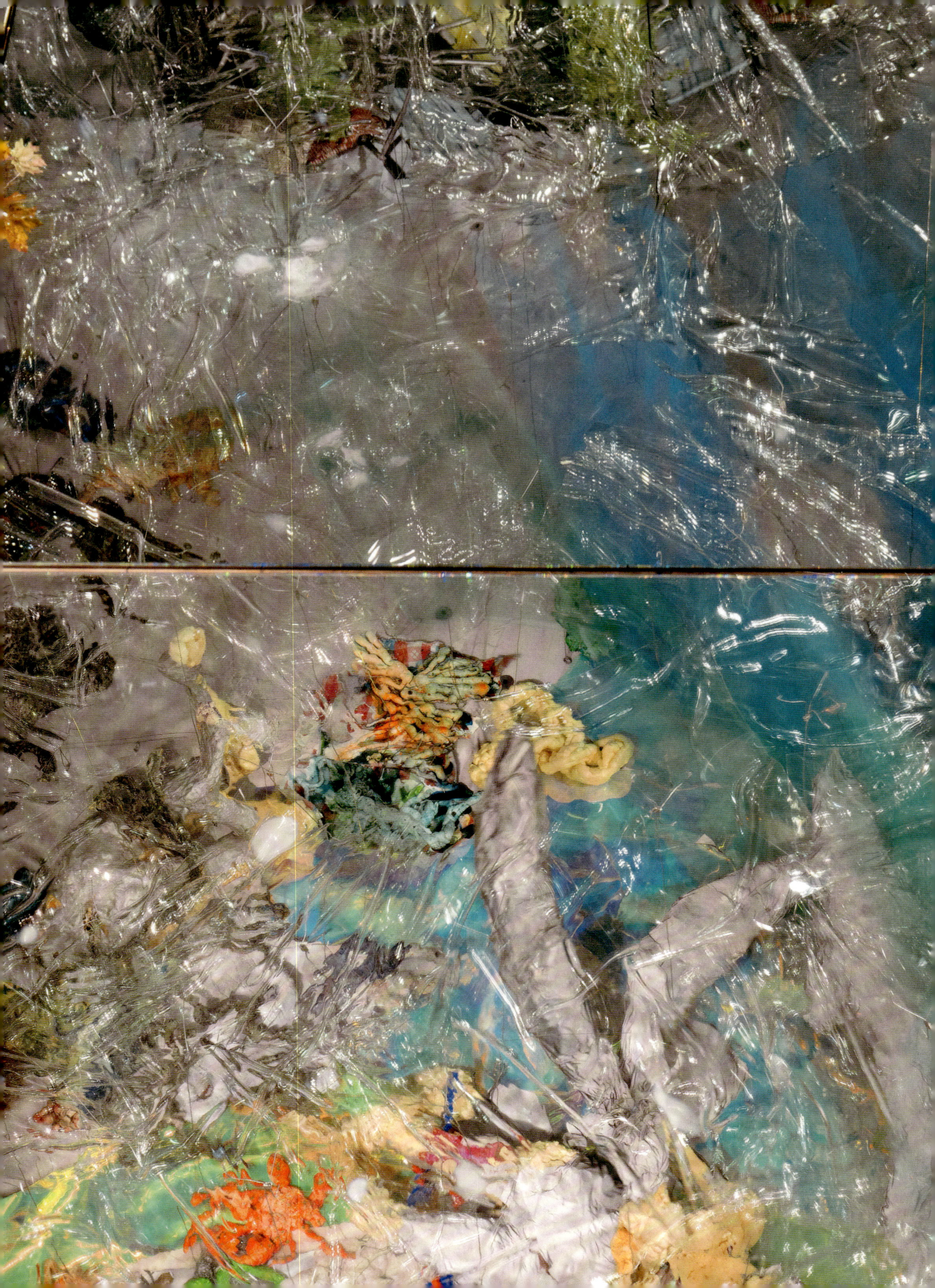

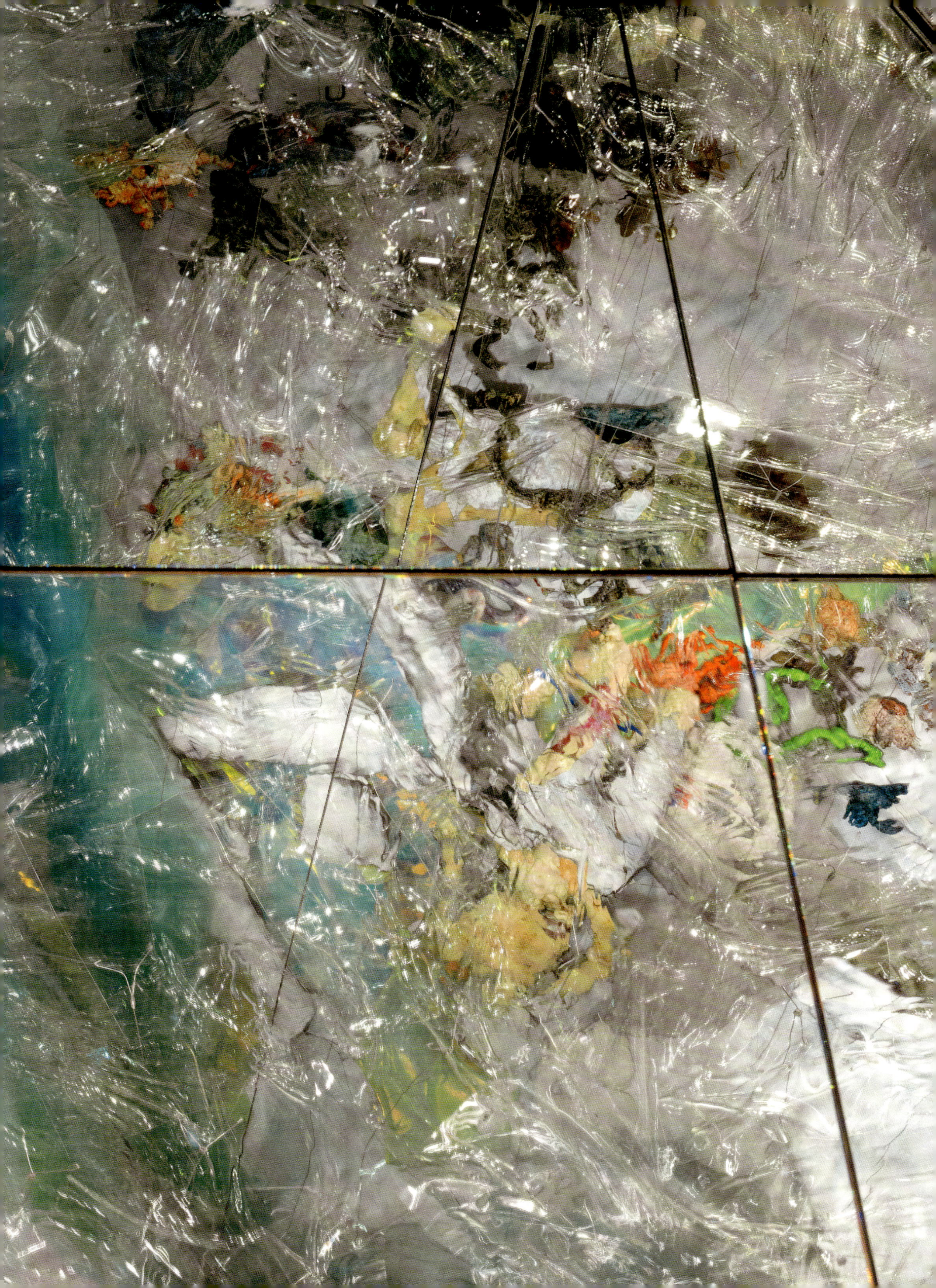

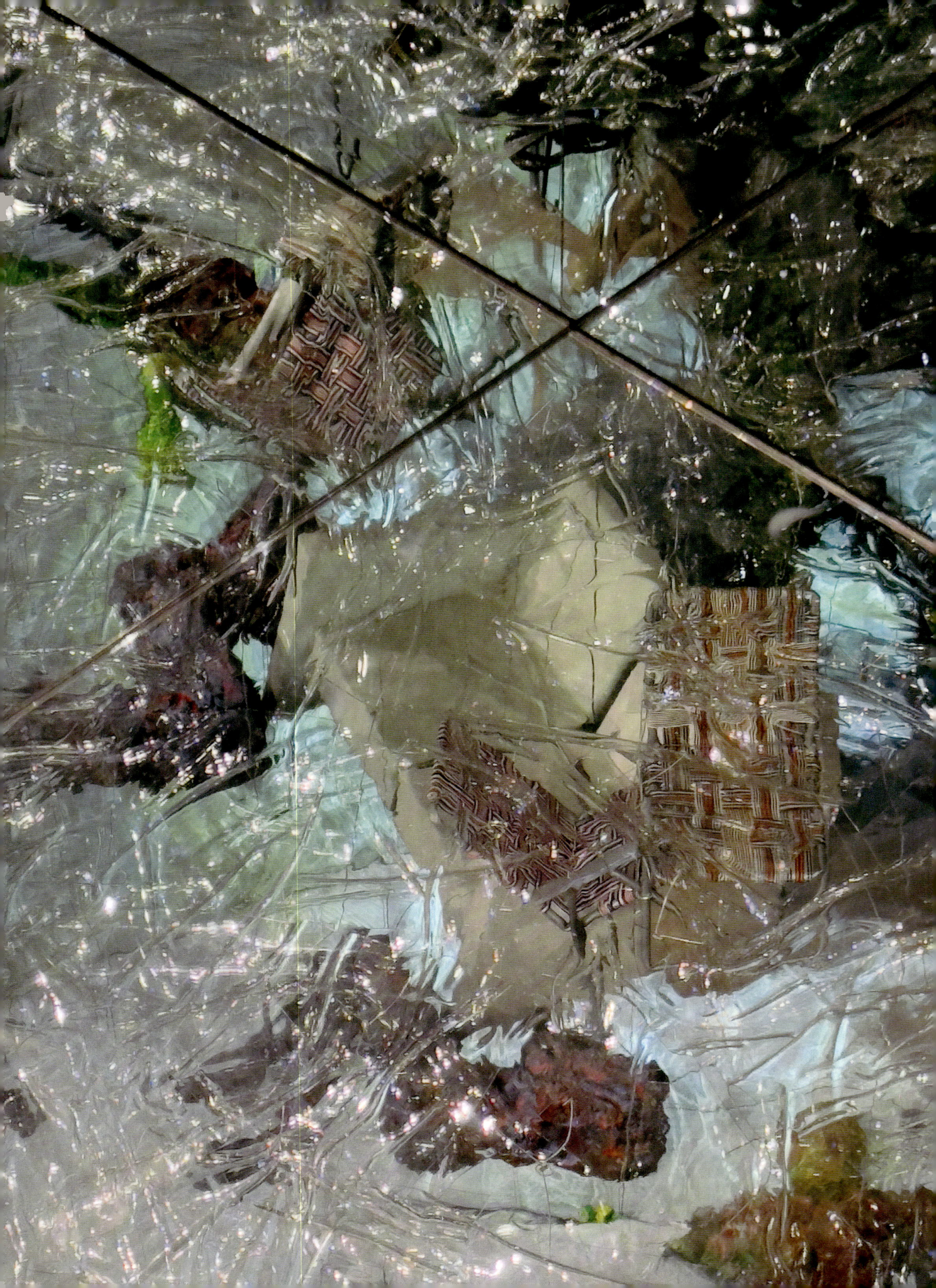

Samara Golden

if earth is the brain then where is the body

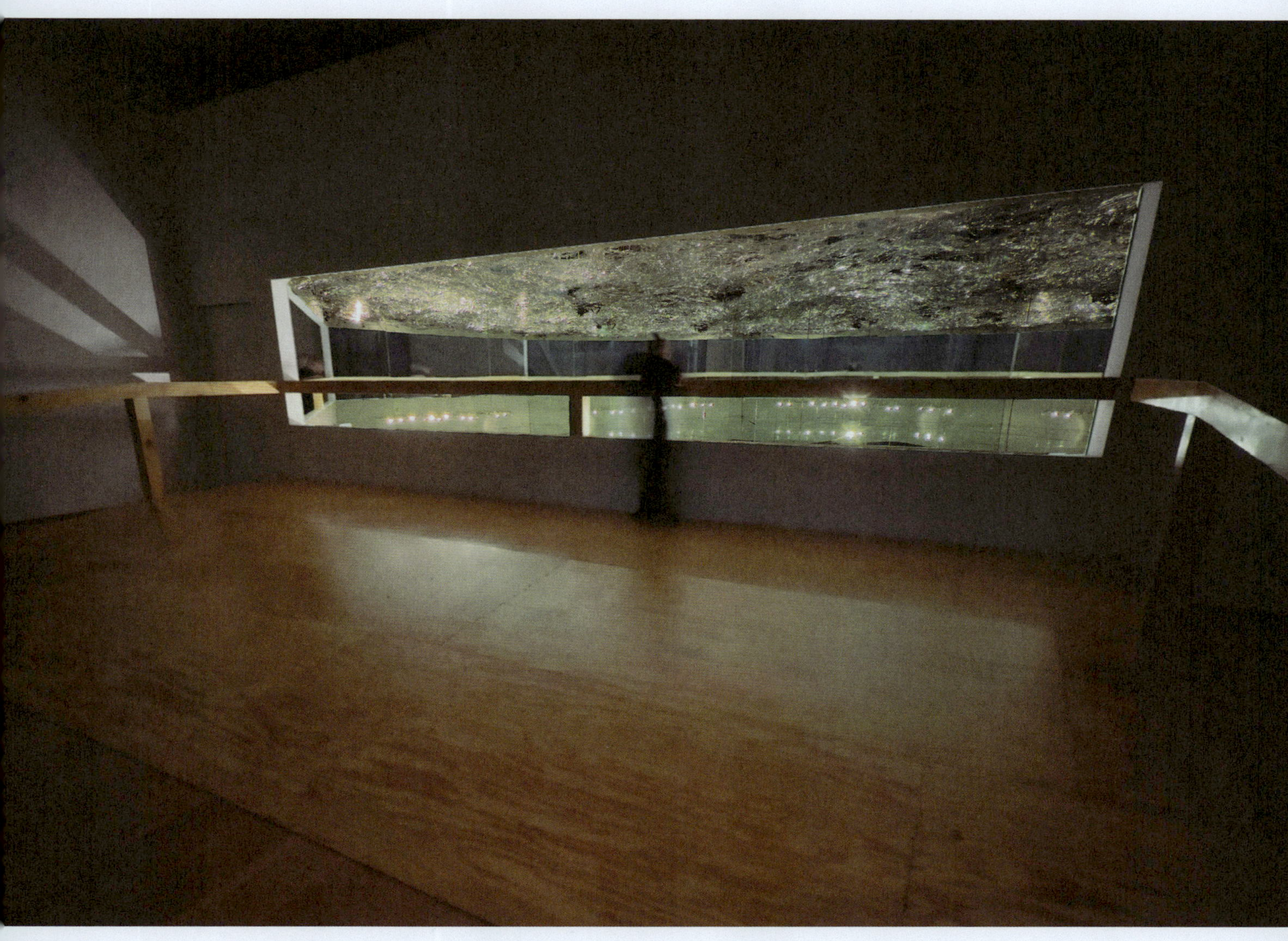

Contents

Foreword and Acknowledgments

Jed Morse

INTERIM DIRECTOR AND

CHIEF CURATOR

Since opening in 2003, the Nasher Sculpture Center has hosted exhibitions of contemporary art that have explored, challenged, and expanded the very definition of sculpture. The museum's building, designed by Renzo Piano, has played no small role in these projects, with artists looking to its signature characteristics as starting points for their interventions. Nairy Baghramian and Otobong Nkanga, for example, suspended works from the steel and glass ceiling of the ground floor galleries. Eva Rothschild made a network of painted pipes that snaked over the admissions desk and down the stairs. Katharina Grosse created a monumental Styrofoam sculpture that appeared to penetrate one of the windows and filled a gallery with dirt, which she then painted. Martin Creed filled the same gallery with balloons, as did Phyllida Barlow with a legion of banners. These last three installations were presented in the Nasher's Lower Level Gallery, whose white walls, glass front, and appealing proportions have brought out the experimental instincts in a number of artists.

Few have so utterly transformed this space as Samara Golden did for *if earth is the brain then where is the body*, her 2024 exhibition. Upon entering the space, visitors ascended a low ramp and took in an utterly astonishing sight: they seemed to be standing at a handrail before a large body of water buffeted by waves and populated by human figures, dolphins, sharks, and other sea life. Golden worked her magic not through sophisticated, high-tech means but with an array of materials readily available at hardware or craft stores: spray insulation foam, paint, insulation panels, fake plants, and electric fans. Making virtually all the sculptural elements herself is an important part of her practice, and the result of these labors were arranged in a room within the gallery, built according to her specifications, whose walls and floor were lined with mirrors. The reflections multiplied its impact, yielding a refracted, dazzling microcosm.

Golden's piece was less a realistic illusion than an evocation—a dreamlike space visitors could mentally traverse, taking in details and watching the changing light on the waves. Water presents strong personal and cultural associations, from paradise to nightmare, and *if earth is the brain then where is the body* seemed to touch upon this range of possibilities. Its multivalent registers of potential meanings continued the concerns of her earlier works but took on a wholly new direction. Prior to this work, made specifically for the Nasher's gallery, she had structured her pieces as architectural spaces. Water had been a noticeable element throughout—perhaps a nod to Golden's adopted home of Los Angeles—but this was the first time she had created such an environment. We are delighted to have hosted this expansion of her practice.

As is often the case when an artist creates new work for an exhibition, the publication devoted to it arrives after the show has already closed. The work's genesis also marks an institutional transition. The project began under the Nasher's previous Director, Jeremy Strick, when he and Senior Curator Dr. Catherine Craft discovered that they shared an enthusiasm for Golden's work. His thoughtfulness, insightful guidance, and innate sympathy for artists exploring new paths laid a solid foundation for what was to come, and we are deeply grateful to him.

Strick retired just before the exhibition opened, and I took on the role of Interim Director. As this book goes to print, the Nasher begins an exciting new chapter, welcoming Carlos Basualdo as its new Director, while I gratefully return to being its Chief Curator.

The exhibition and publication have benefited from the support of a diverse array of individuals and institutions. I would like to thank Frost Bank for its leading support of the exhibition. The Dallas Art Fair Foundation provided additional assistance. We are grateful as well for the generous support of the Dallas Tourism Public Improvement District (DTPID), Miyoung Lee, Karen Hillenburg, Carole Server, and Irwin N. Gold Family Foundation.

This publication marks a significant contribution to the understanding of Golden's work. Dr. Craft, curator of the exhibition, served as the editor of this volume and has contributed an extensive essay that offers new insights into the artist's practice. Working with her was the remarkable Nasher team:

Head Registrar Carra Henry, Associate Registrar Shelby Zhu, Head Preparator Courtney Stembridge, Conservator Claire Taggart, and Conservation Lab Technician Nicole Berastequi. Curator Dr. Leigh Arnold lent insights and support, as did Curatorial Assistant Sydney Smith. Educational programs were developed for this exhibition by Curator of Education Anna Smith, as well as Manager of School and Family Programs Sarah Janke and Manager of Access and Outreach Programs Lynda Wilbur. Marketing, publicity, and events were capably overseen by Director of External Affairs Jill Magnuson, working with Manager of Communications and International Programs Adrienne Lichliter-Hines, Social Media Manager Emma Ahmad, Marketing Manager Molly Sydnor, Senior Graphic Designer Jamie Huckaby, Senior Manager of Emerging Technologies and Evaluation Jacques Haba, Manager of Strategic Events and Programming Lindsey James, External Affairs Project Manager Kirsten MacIntosh, Manager of Visitor Experiences Isabel Lee-Rosson, and Assistant Manager of Visitor Experiences Mary Poole. Fundraising efforts were overseen by Co-Director of Development for Individual Giving David Leggett and Co-Director of Development for Institutional Giving Vanessa Hadox, Manager of Institutional Giving Cale Peterson, Manager of Membership and Individual Giving Susan Stout, Manager of Development Communications Devin Berg, and Manager of Development Operations Cameron Casey. Deputy Director of Finance and Operations John McBride and Senior Accountant Jennifer Lyons made certain that the project's financial needs ran smoothly. From the Director's office, Executive Assistant and Patron Travel Coordinator Amy Henry worked with all members of our team. Operations Manager Chris Bosco contributed his deep knowledge of our facility and oversaw the construction of the exhibition structure to assure an efficient process for the installation.

Our deepest thanks go to Samara Golden for her collaboration with us on this project. Her visionary creation of an extraordinary work fascinated viewers and offered so many ways to consider our relationship with one of the earth's most familiar, and most precious, resources.

Samara Golden, *if earth is the brain then where is the body*, 2024.
Glass mirror, clear plastic, XPS foam board, spray foam, acrylic paint,
reflective fabric, dichroic vinyl, fabric, lighting gels, found objects,
wire, rope, and fans; 22 × 27 × 15 ft. (6.7 × 8.2 × 4.5 m).

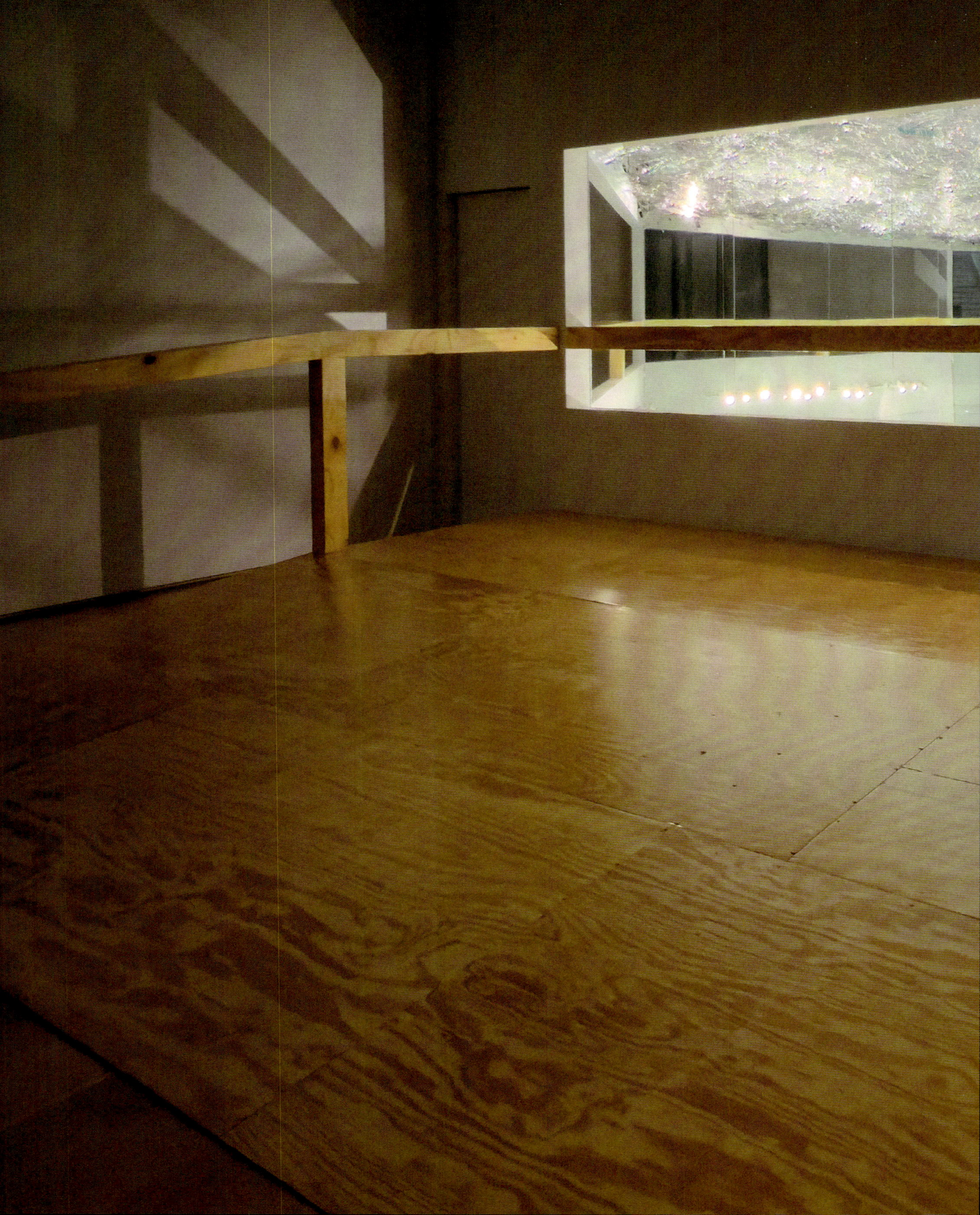

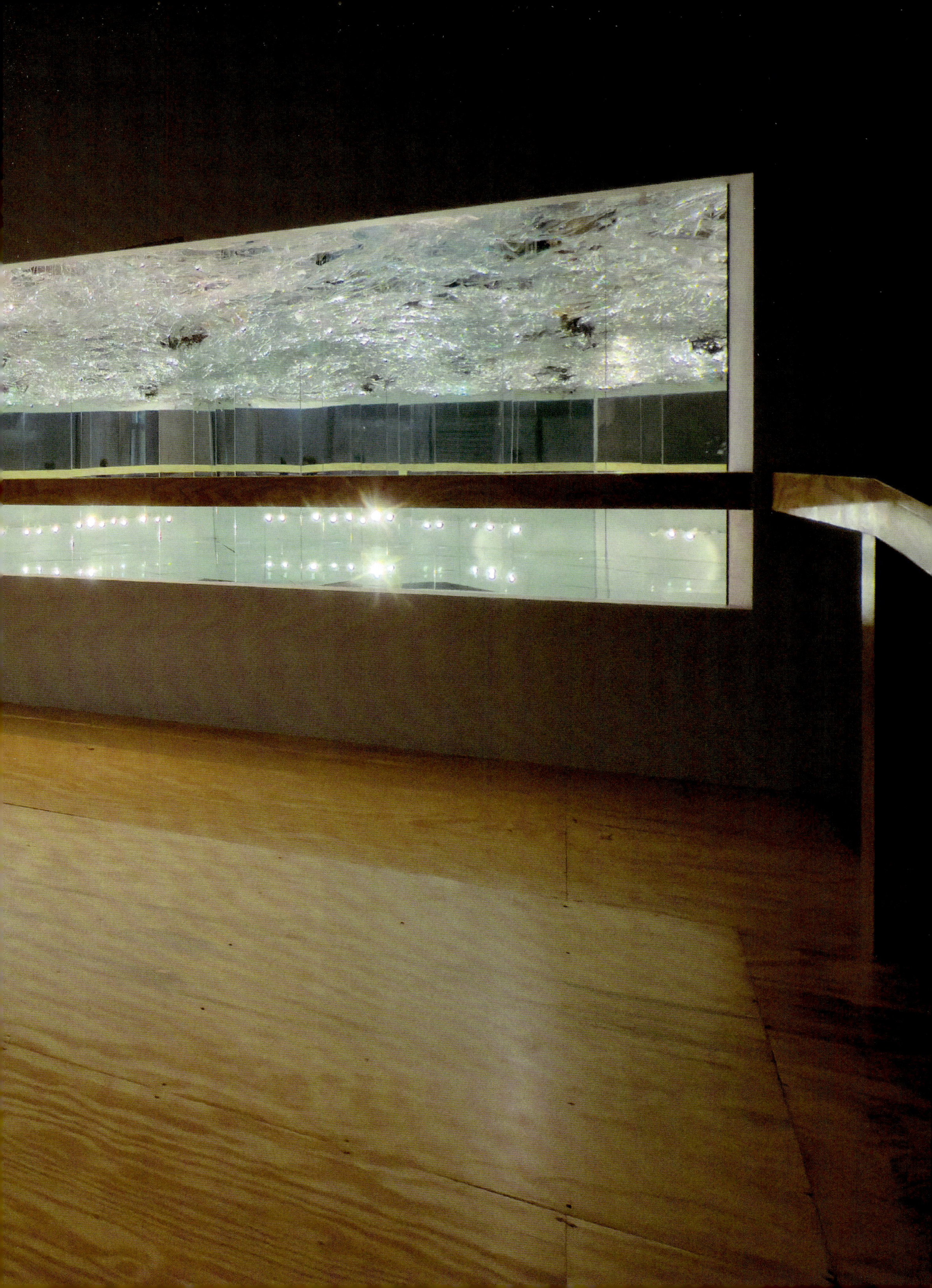

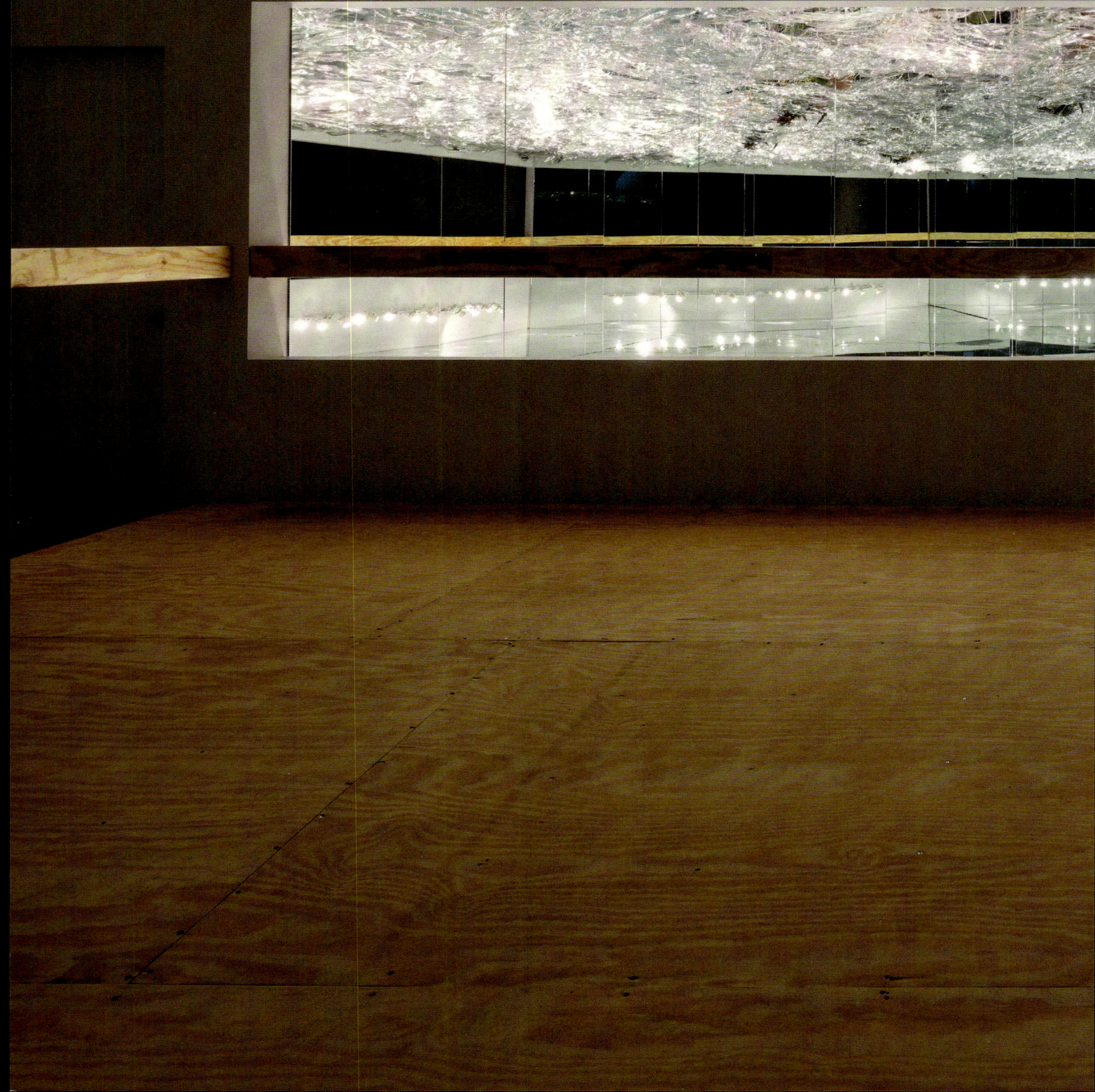

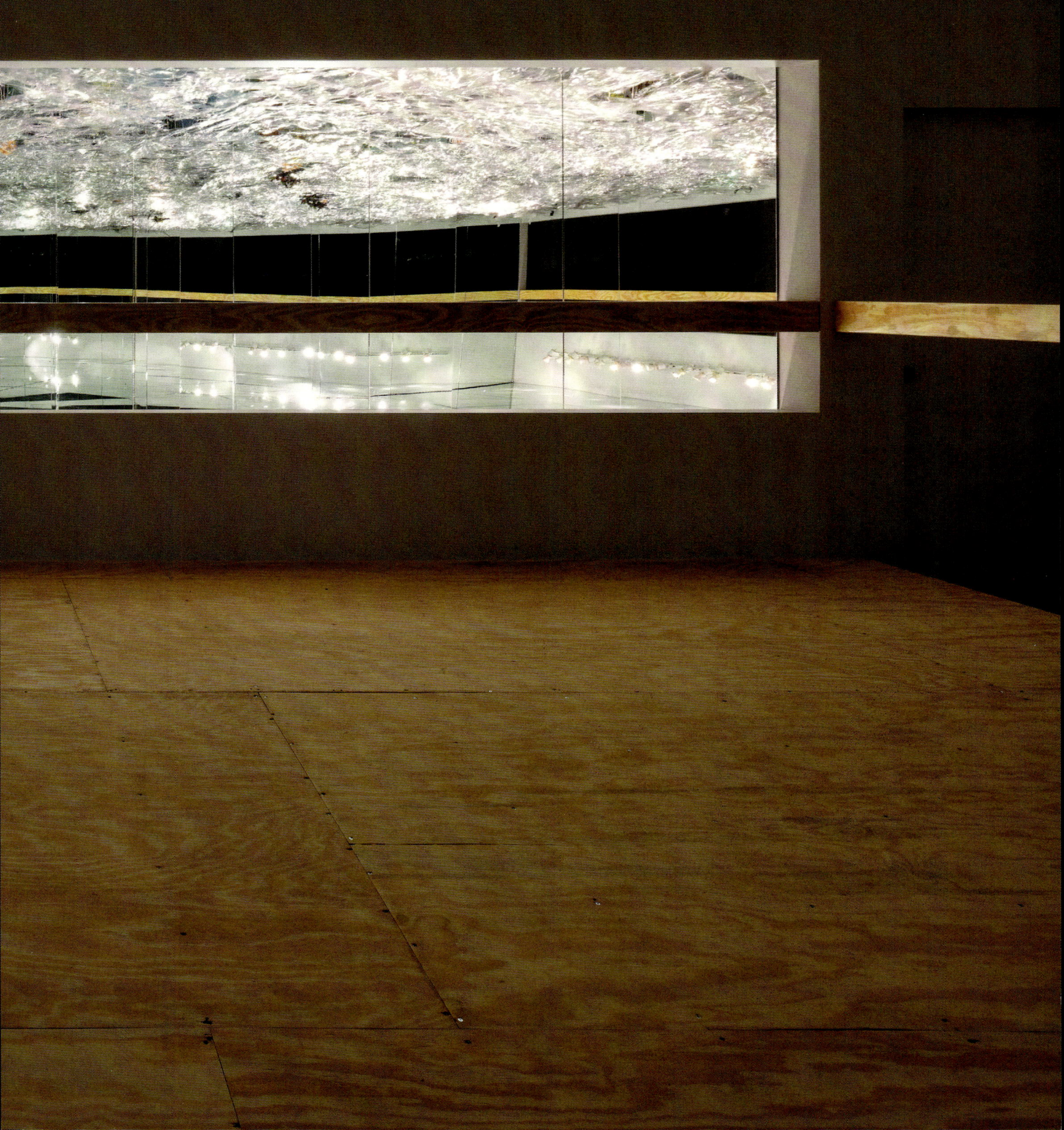

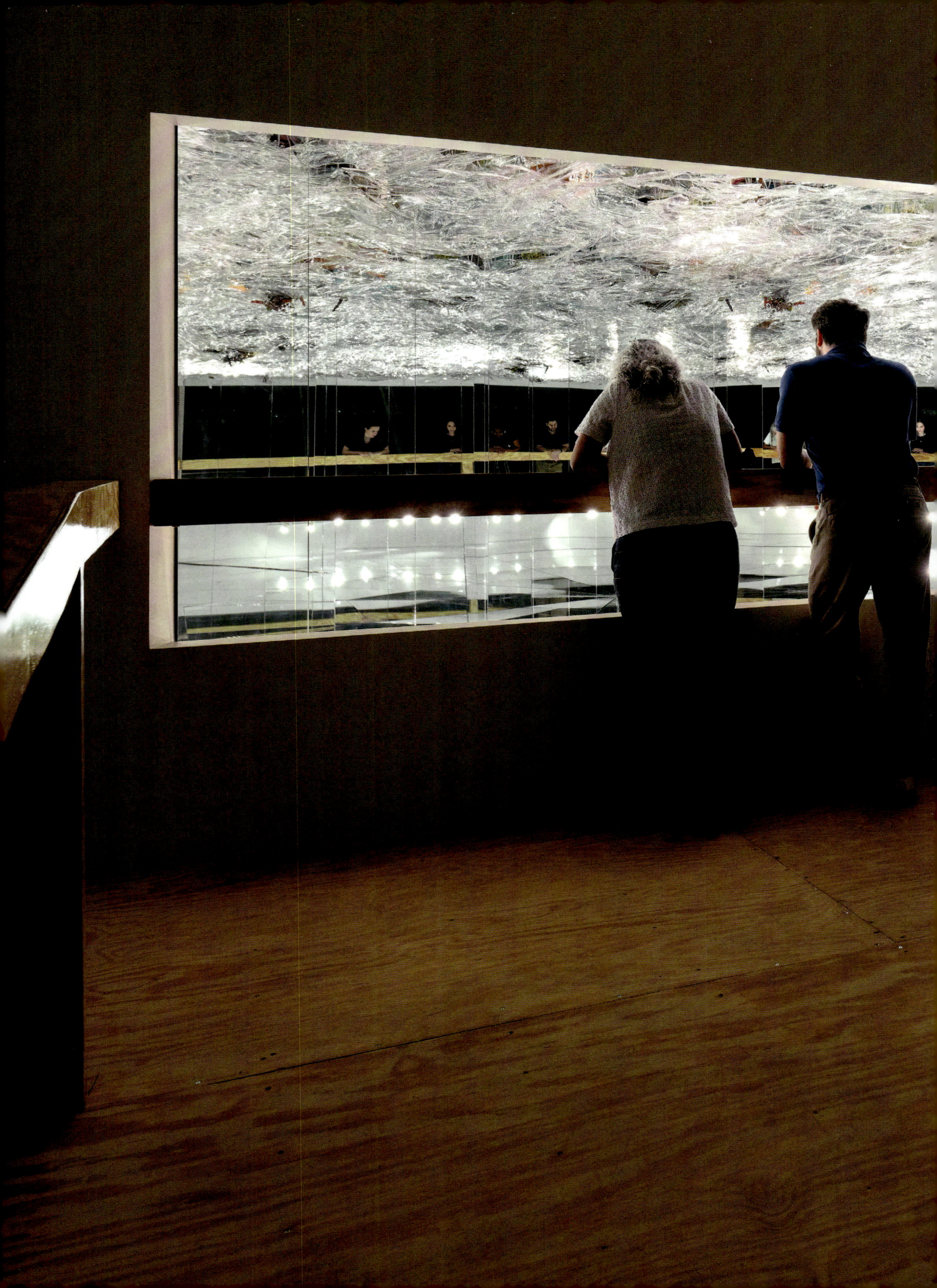

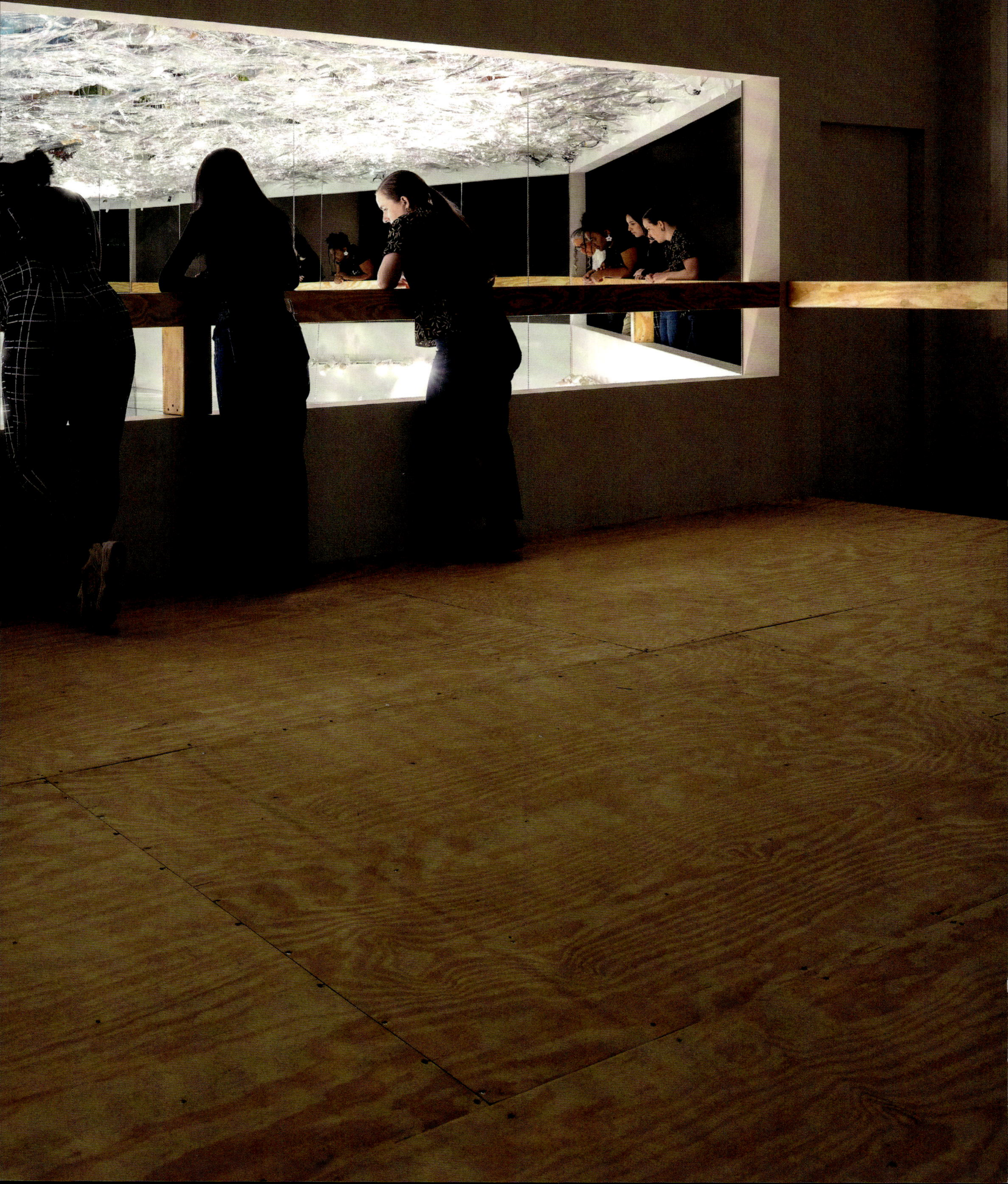

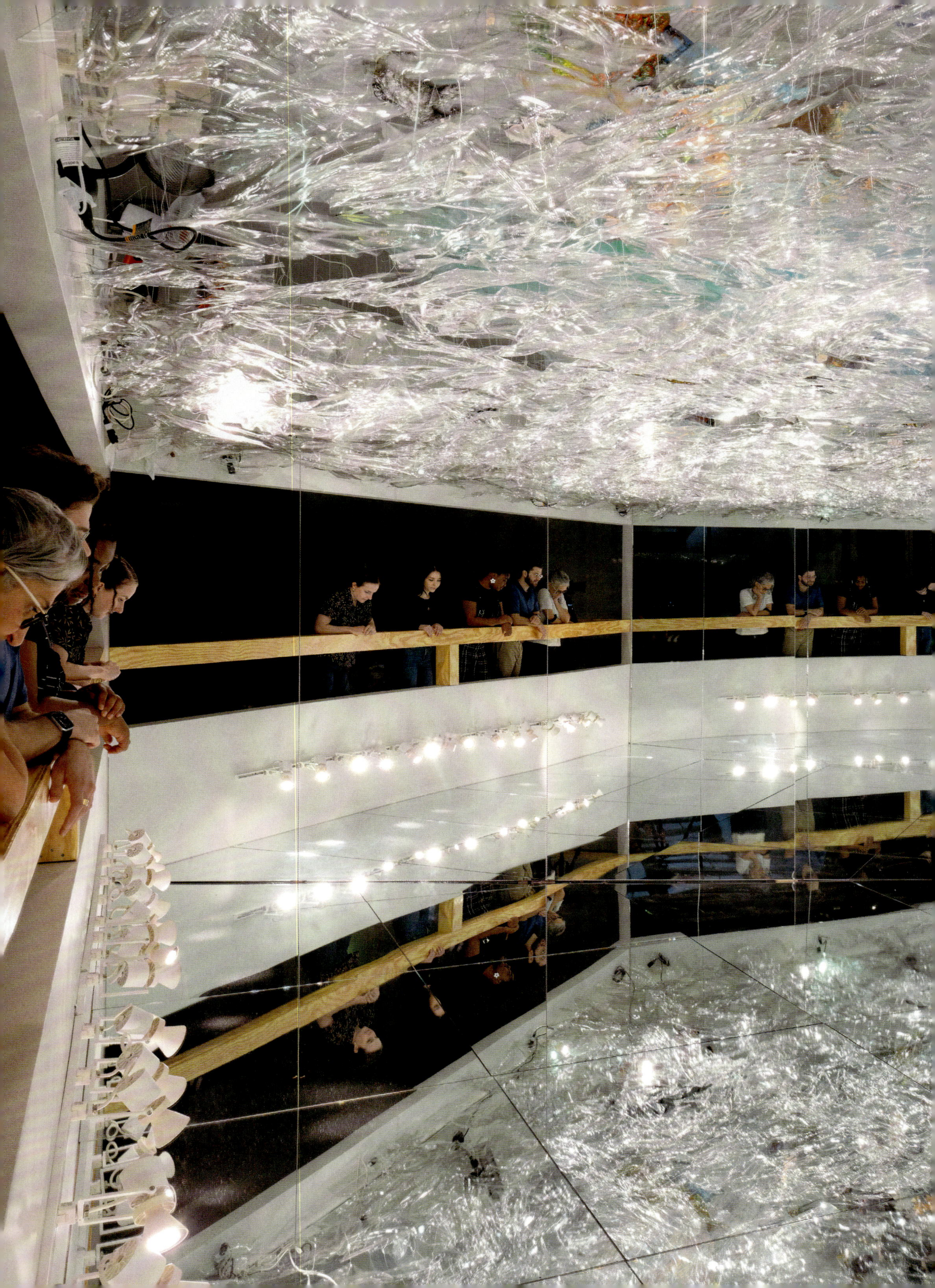

a convening

CATHERINE CRAFT

25

Light defines the Nasher Sculpture Center. With its armature of steel and glass, the building offers the impression of a museum without a roof. Natural light suffuses the main floor, with large dual staircases near the admission desks descending to a lower level. At the foot of the stairs, visitors stand before a gallery whose glass doors and large windows reveal that it lacks the rest of the building's characteristic travertine cladding. The architect Renzo Piano and his patron, Raymond Nasher, envisioned it as an intimately scaled space for smaller artworks. As contemporary artists began to contribute to the museum's program, the gallery took on the character of a white cube, in Brian O'Doherty's sense—a site for installations that could be anywhere and yet nowhere else, with the bonus of offering a spectacular view from the staircase landing.[1]

Occasionally, artists have shunned the spectacle of that reveal. Mai-Thu Perret used Vaseline, an old cinematic trick (FIG. 1), on some of the windows, while Michael Dean whitewashed them. Samara Golden's predecessor in this gallery, Sarah Sze, had the

FIG. 1. Installation view, *Sightings: Mai-Thu Perret*

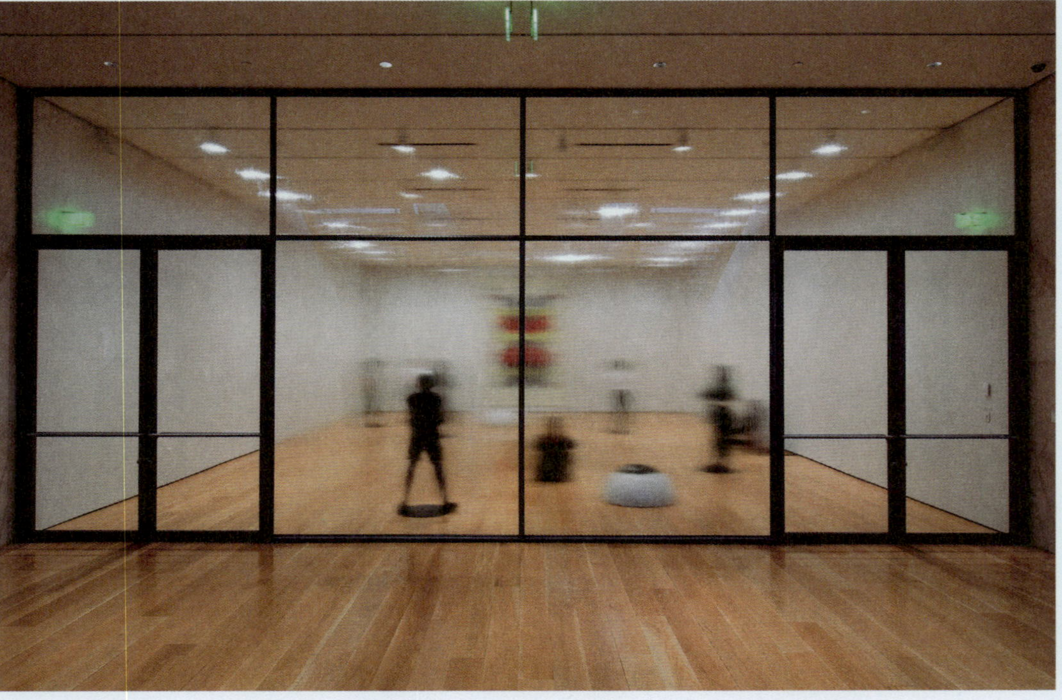

windows coated with a reflective, translucent vinyl that caught images of a rotating projection within while slightly dimming the environment. In each case, thwarting the view into the gallery through the glass kept alive an element of surprise, resulting in a somewhat theatrical environment, with freestanding elements staged as figures of human presence.[2]

For her Nasher presentation, Golden added a layer of even darker vinyl to Sze's covering, yet the result was not charcoal blankness. Instead, faint, haloed bleeds of light, some swaying or twinkling, seeped through, visible to anyone descending the stairs. One could see that there was *something* in there, but its identity was not clear, nor was the type of space containing it. Context called for an artwork; the flickering glow, shaped in a circling arc, implied some more infernal identity, sunk into the core of the building's foundation.

layers

Golden wanted this darkness as "a way to emphasize what's inside," to allow visitors "to forget about the outside," and to generate "a shift of attention" upon entering the gallery. If the exterior view obscured and the interior darkened, it was "what the piece wanted."[3] Yet she also recognized that the dimness—when glimpsed from the outside, before entering the gallery—evoked the impression of an industrial area, not a space for art. In fact, this experience hinted at an aspect of the building's design that was unknown to the artist: behind the gallery, hidden to the public, runs a long corridor that houses the museum's heating and cooling systems, a gray network of concrete and steel generators and pipes. Also unknown to the artist while she worked out the watery concept for her exhibition was another unseen element: a buried stream of water courses under the museum's garden—a branch of the Trinity River sent underground in the early twentieth century.[4]

This constellation of happenstance is appropriate, for Golden's art has long been one of layers, seen and unseen, literal and conjured. Perhaps the most enigmatic element of her work is its imperviousness to description. Knowing how it is made—having seen it made, in my case—does nothing to lessen its unexpected, even confounding effects. To view Golden's work at the Nasher, upon entering the Lower Level Gallery, visitors ascended a wide ramp leading to a handrail that marked a modestly elevated lookout onto the piece. What they were seeing, likely without realizing it, was a room shaped like a generous wedge of pie that had been built within the gallery by contractors according to the artist's specifications. Its walls and floor were covered with large sheets of quarter-inch mirror. On the ceiling the artist, assisted by four art handlers provided by the museum, attached elements in three strata. First were sheets of stiff foam covered in a gray reflective fabric that seemed to change colors depending on the light it received. To these panels Golden attached sculptural elements, made primarily from spray insulation that she had painted in bright colors, similarly manufactured to trap and refract light. The outermost layer was a series of clear plastic squares, each warped with a heat gun and suspended from the ceiling to create the impression of transparent, if reflective, waves.

These elements multiplied in the triangulation of the inward-facing mirrors, where they seemed to merge into a single environment that appeared to be a large body of water with a variety of denizens "beneath" the waves. There were additional, animating layers that Golden spent as much time installing and adjusting as what most of us might consider the artwork proper—that is, its physical elements. She placed lights above and below the handrail and above the wedge's point at the back of the gallery; to a few of these she added green or blue gels. In addition to the practical necessity of illuminating the installation, the lights activated the reflective fabrics and paints, which could in turn appear as differently colored, depending upon the viewer's position along the handrail or indeed which reflection of an object was being seen. Above the top row of lights she mounted a half-dozen fans, several of which oscillated. These stirred lights that were suspended from power cords as well as the squares of plastic, so that they (and some of the looser elements affixed to the ceiling) appeared to sway and undulate. The oscillating drone of the fans added an auditory element, suggesting an environment both natural and industrial.

intuition

The installation process progressed logically, to a point. The room was constructed, the walls were lined with mirrors, and the fabric-covered panels were placed in the ceiling. One might next expect the sculptural elements to be attached to these panels, but instead Golden installed the clear plastic squares, hanging them on wires four feet below the ceiling; she then lit the squares and animated them with fans. This meant that the sculptural elements had to be attached to the ceiling by first parting the squares of plastic. Before the mirrored floor was added, large squares of mirror on dollies were rolled about to gauge details of the larger composition taking shape, as Golden had not worked out the overall arrangement in advance. Its creation instead took place as the work was installed, often requiring the artist to toggle back and forth between setting sculptures, then (re)adjusting lights and fans.

I asked Golden why she was installing the plastic squares first when, without them in the way, attaching the sculptural elements to the ceiling would have undoubtedly been easier. She explained that since she had never attempted to create a body of water in her art, she was not sure that it would work. Before anything else, she needed to see the waves in place, then in motion, to know that it looked like, or even approximated, what she had envisioned—what she had created, in a much smaller section, in her studio. Only then could she proceed to populate its depths.

Intuition is not commonly mentioned in writings on contemporary sculpture. Unquantifiable and unprovable, its traces linger just below the surface of discourse. Yet artists can have this uncanny, lucky sense that lets them reach beyond themselves to pick up, unknowingly, on aspects of context and meaning. This may be what Golden means when she uses the word "witchy" in conversation to refer to elements of the creative process that remain mysterious even to her. With her inversion of the logical way to proceed—to work from the ceiling down until the waves were placed and activated last—Golden instead inadvertently echoed a series of primal myths. She created a world that began with the earth and the heavens, followed by a body of water animated by light and wind, and lastly populated with sea life, plants, and humans and their detritus. With the addition of the mirrored floor, the world was complete: a roughly circular expanse of water, teeming with more than could be recognized or named. To all of it, Golden gave a title that came to her, unbidden, in what she saw as "part of a fluid ongoing thought": *if earth is the brain then where is the body*.[5]

looking down, looking back

Golden's realization of her exhibition's title marked a transition. Artists often name a work only after the laborious work of its conception is complete. Provided just before traveling to Dallas to begin installation, *if earth is the brain then where is the body* initiated a more public process of putting words to the art being created. I began the notes for this essay shortly thereafter and continued writing it for several months after the exhibition closed. Mine joins numerous belated texts written for the now-common phenomenon of exhibition catalogues published after shows have come and gone.

Documentation and analysis of new works and commemoration of now-dispersed objects have replaced a book issued in tandem with its subject. In the case of a work such as Golden's, the essay further becomes an account of a time and space that no longer exist: after her exhibition ended, its contents were taken down, and its mirrored chamber was demolished. The artwork endures, transfigured, in this book; the reader's posture—looking downward, into its bound pages—becomes a condensed, visceral echo of the visitor's gaze downward into the installation's mirrored reflections.

Also seen in this book's pages are its arguably more vital elements: photographs of the now-vanished artwork, most of them taken by the artist. Indeed, photography is critical to Golden. Far from regarding her photographs as straightforward documentation, she seems to understand them as another way to experience the work:

> As soon as a show opens, I'm onto the photography immediately; it's about switching gears completely, going from full-on physical materialization to full-on condensing, boiling down, flattening. I like the photographs to be another way to see the work. To me, photos never capture "reality," they make a new reality. There doesn't seem to be a way to record all the specific feeling in the piece, so I like the idea of making the photographs hold some other kind of emotion or confusion that is its own thing.[6]

Compared with the installation proper—that is, as it lingers in my eyewitness memory—Golden's images do indeed "flatten" their subject, perhaps inevitably. Experienced in person, *if earth is the brain then where is the body* did curious things to one's vision, generating a perceptual tug-of-war for attention among its multiple layers. To see it fully required both seeing through the waves to the elements below and a steady attentiveness to the water's surface.

This was surprisingly close to the experience of looking at actual bodies of water, but Golden somehow compressed the sensation, intensified it. Such encounters are almost impossible to record photographically; the cyclopic eye of the camera focuses greedily on the visual noise of the waving surface, no matter how much we want it to follow our own penetrating gaze. Golden's own photographs manage glimpses of both, captured in unexpected flickers of color. Not surprisingly, they resulted from her practice of merging and collaging multiple shots taken under widely varying lighting conditions—photographic images every bit as manipulated and mediated as the installation whose surrogates they have become.

what came before

For nearly fifteen years, Samara Golden has been making installations that create disquieting and disorienting environments. Often populated by figures or traces of their presence, they have in the past spoken to experiences of violence and its aftermath, disparities of class, or illness and recovery. She has often used mirrors in architectural spaces to create mind-bogglingly complex environments that can range from seemingly chaotic to quietly seething. While Golden may populate them with figures, she has often focused on things—office equipment, hospital beds, or the remains of a meal, for example—that suggest a place recently deserted. Each element is typically handmade by the artist, who has reached for materials ranging from Thermax insulation panels and plastics to epoxy and spray foam to construct settings that are both familiar and ill at ease in their artificiality. Her tendency to make these objects at half-scale contributes to the impression that viewers are encountering a vast area.

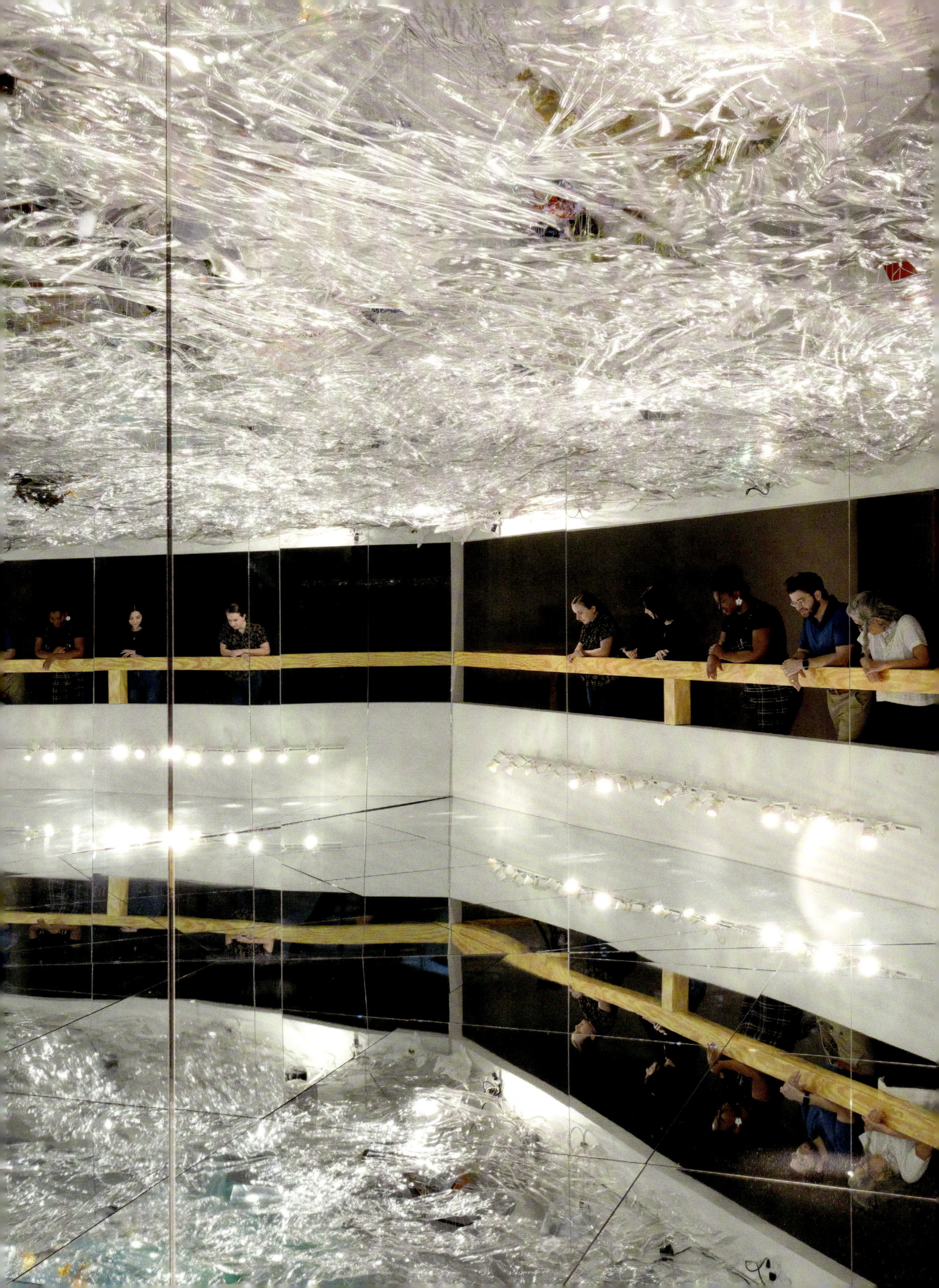

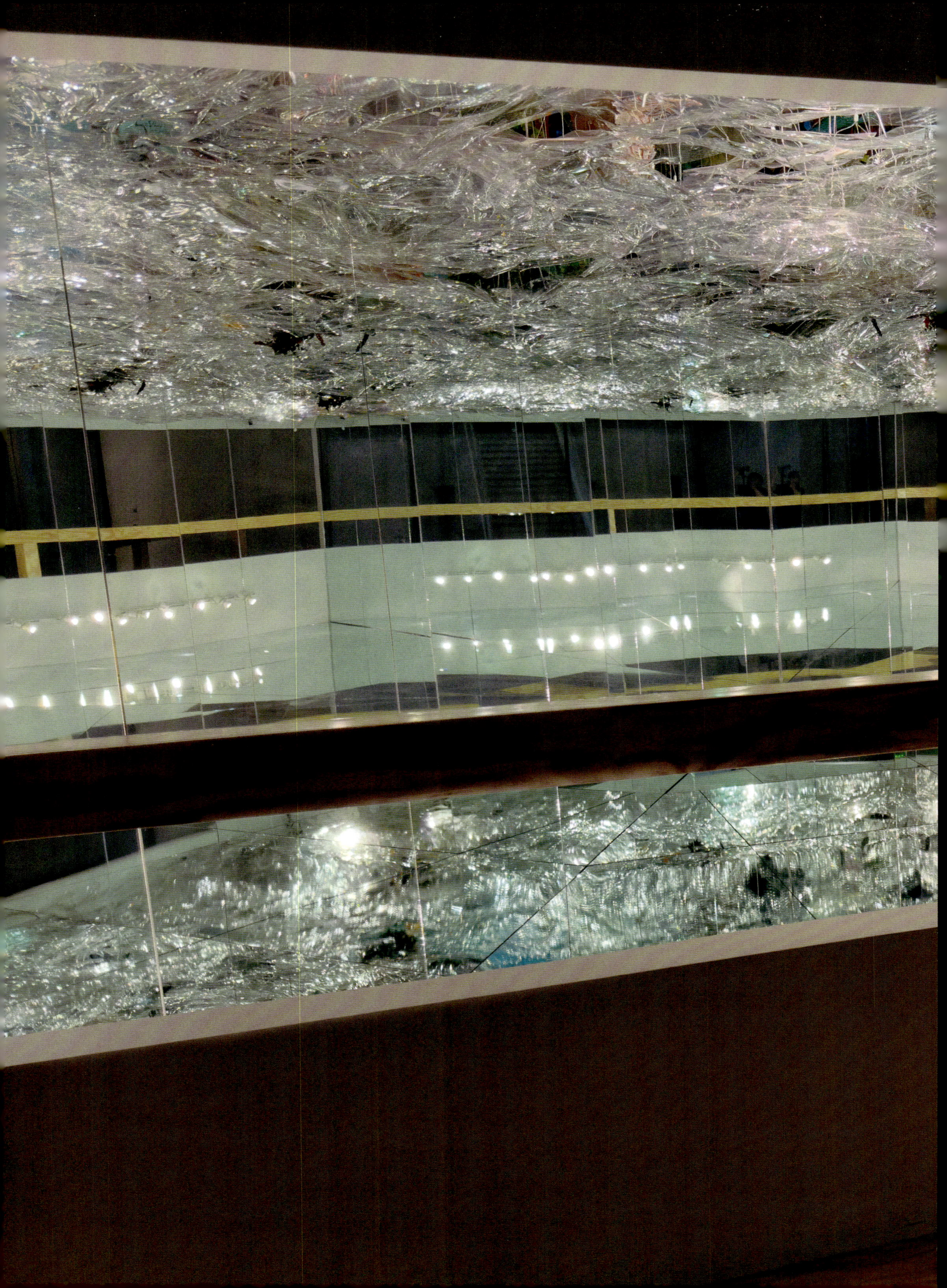

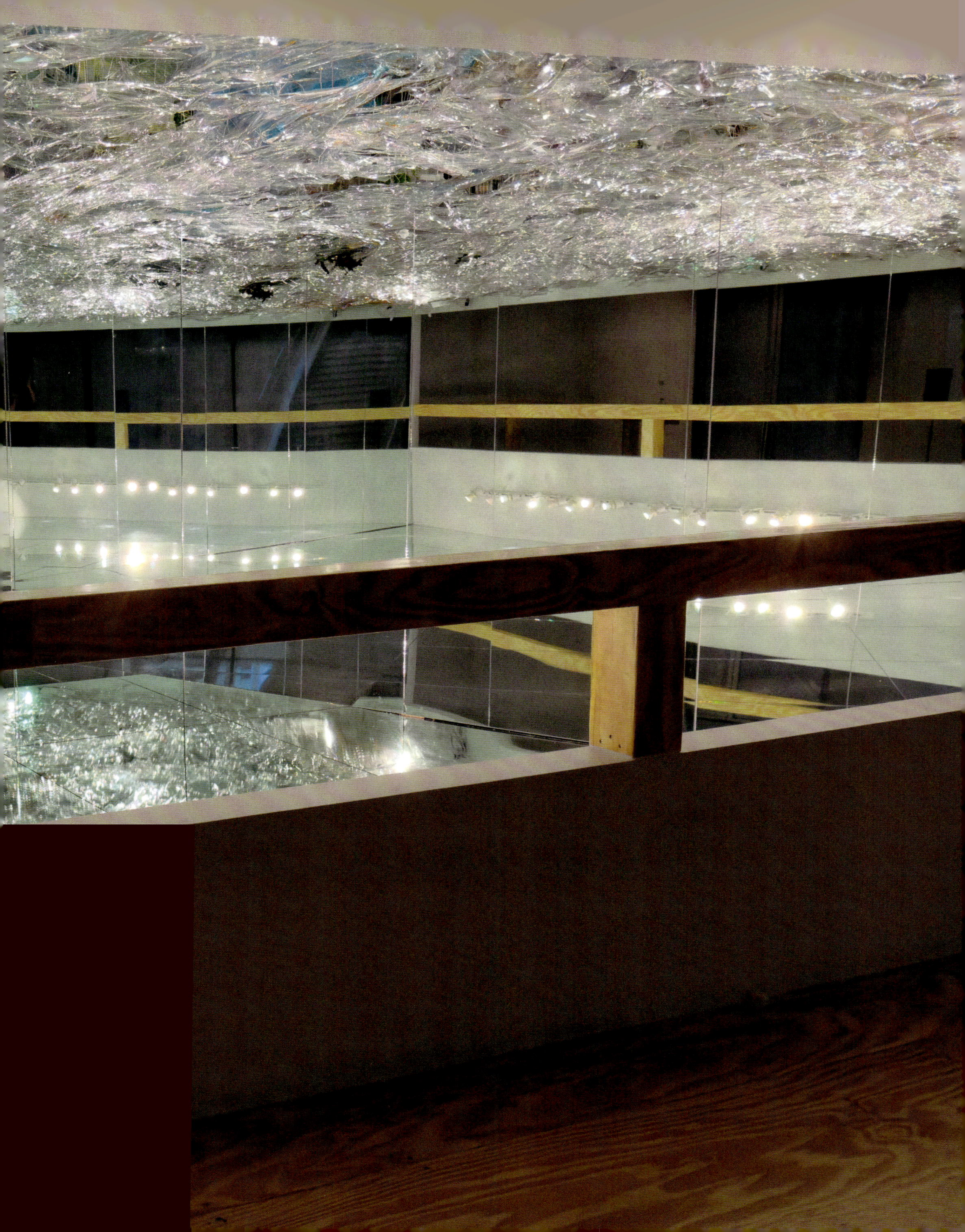

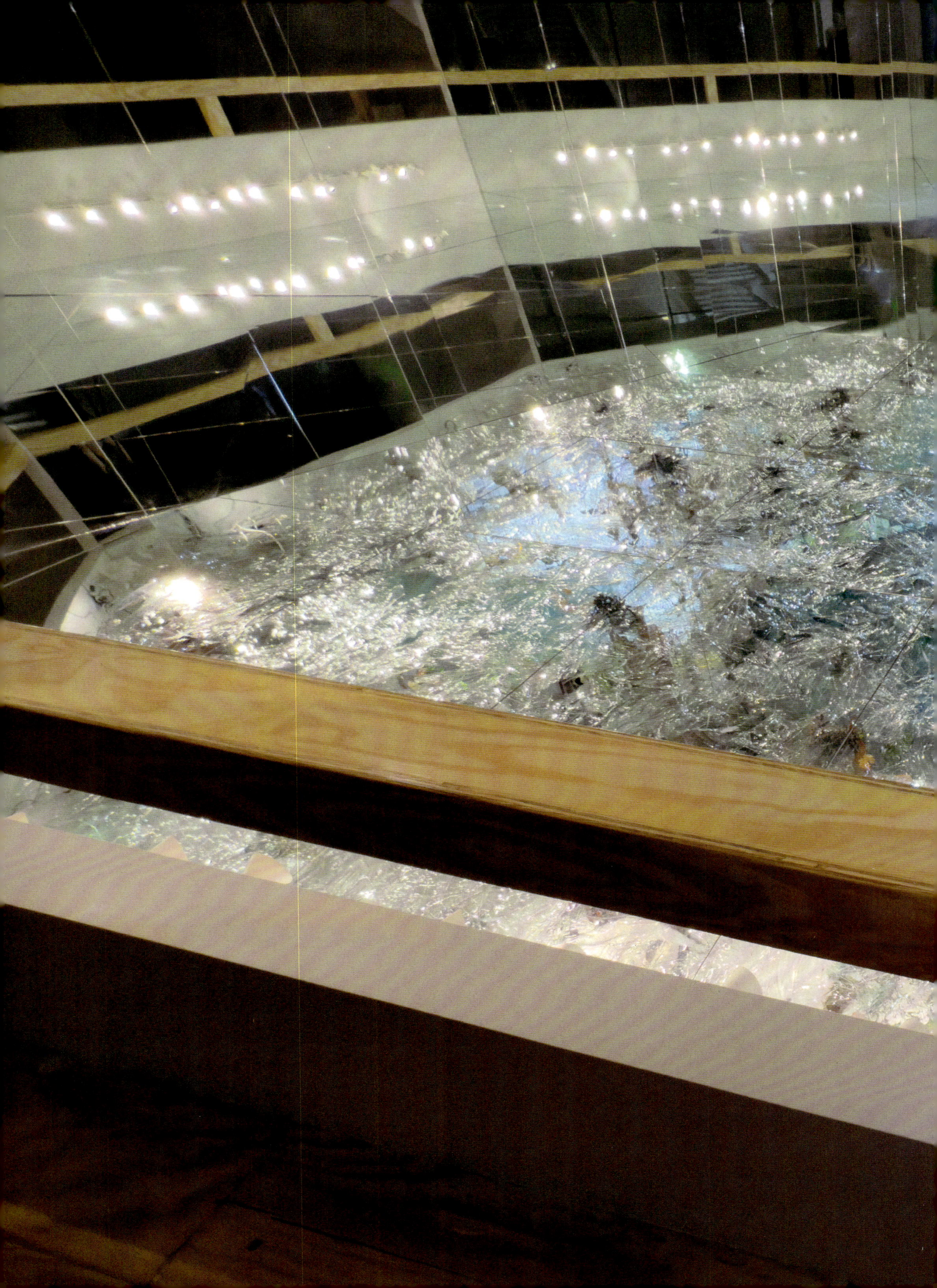

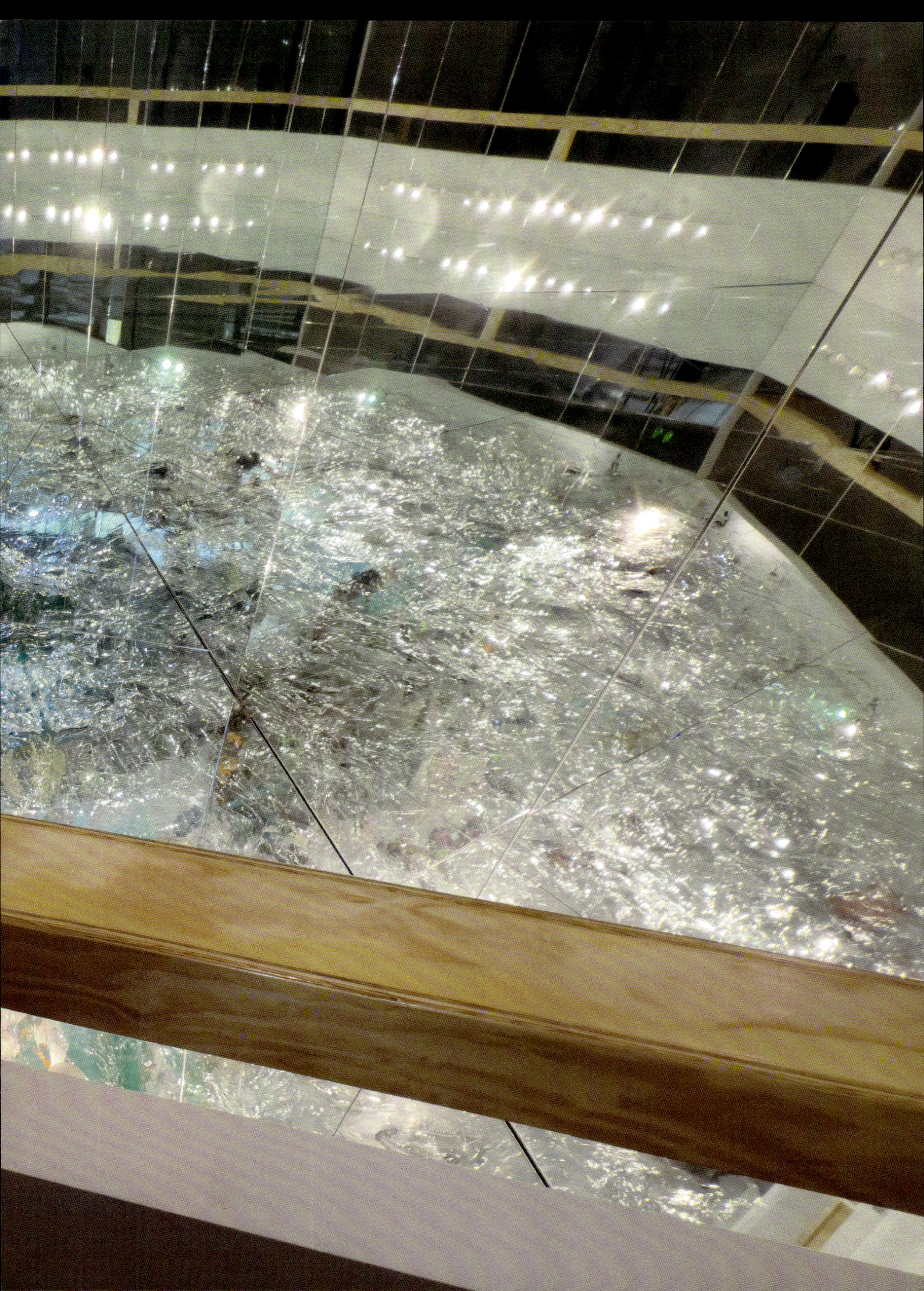

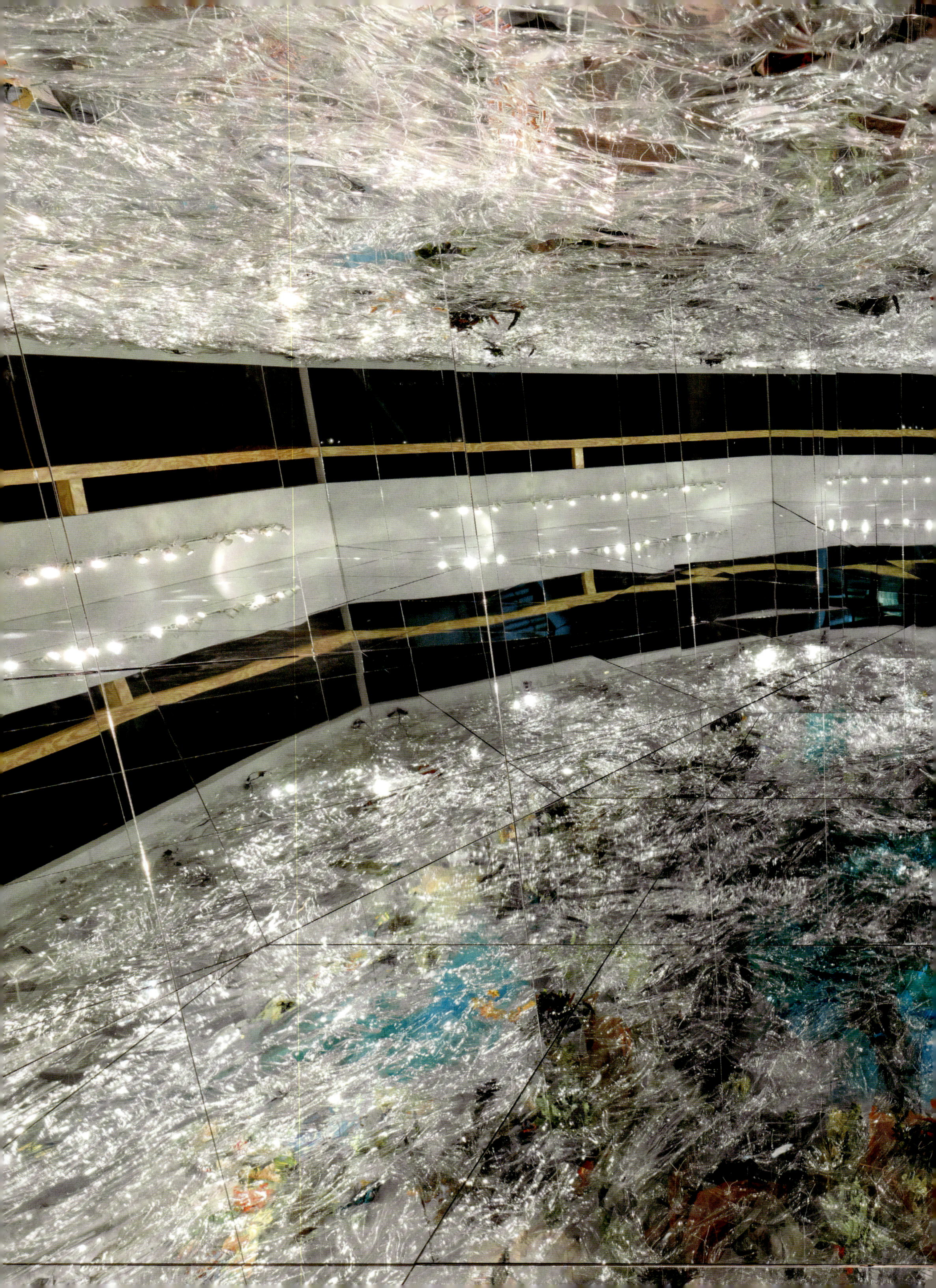

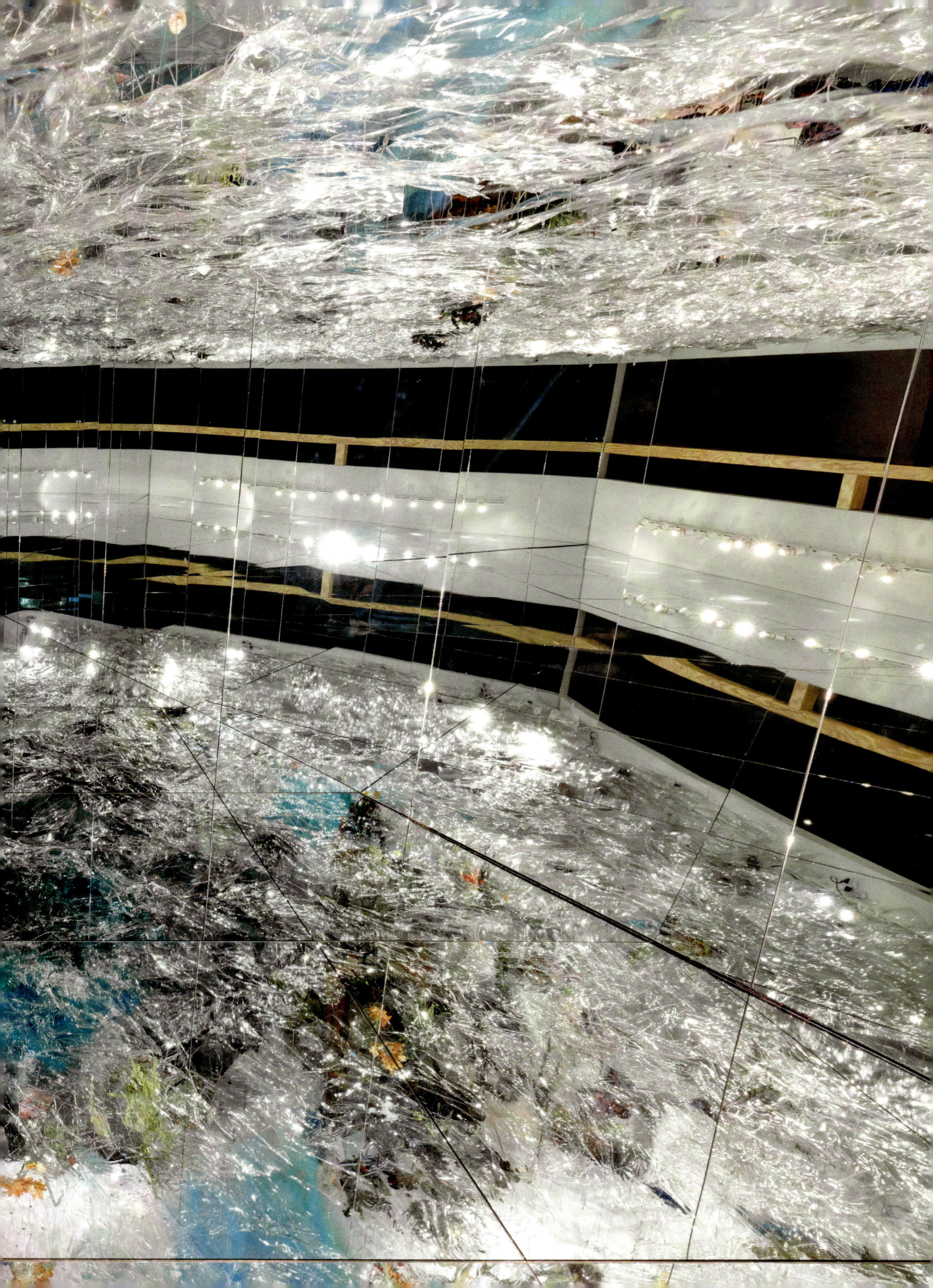

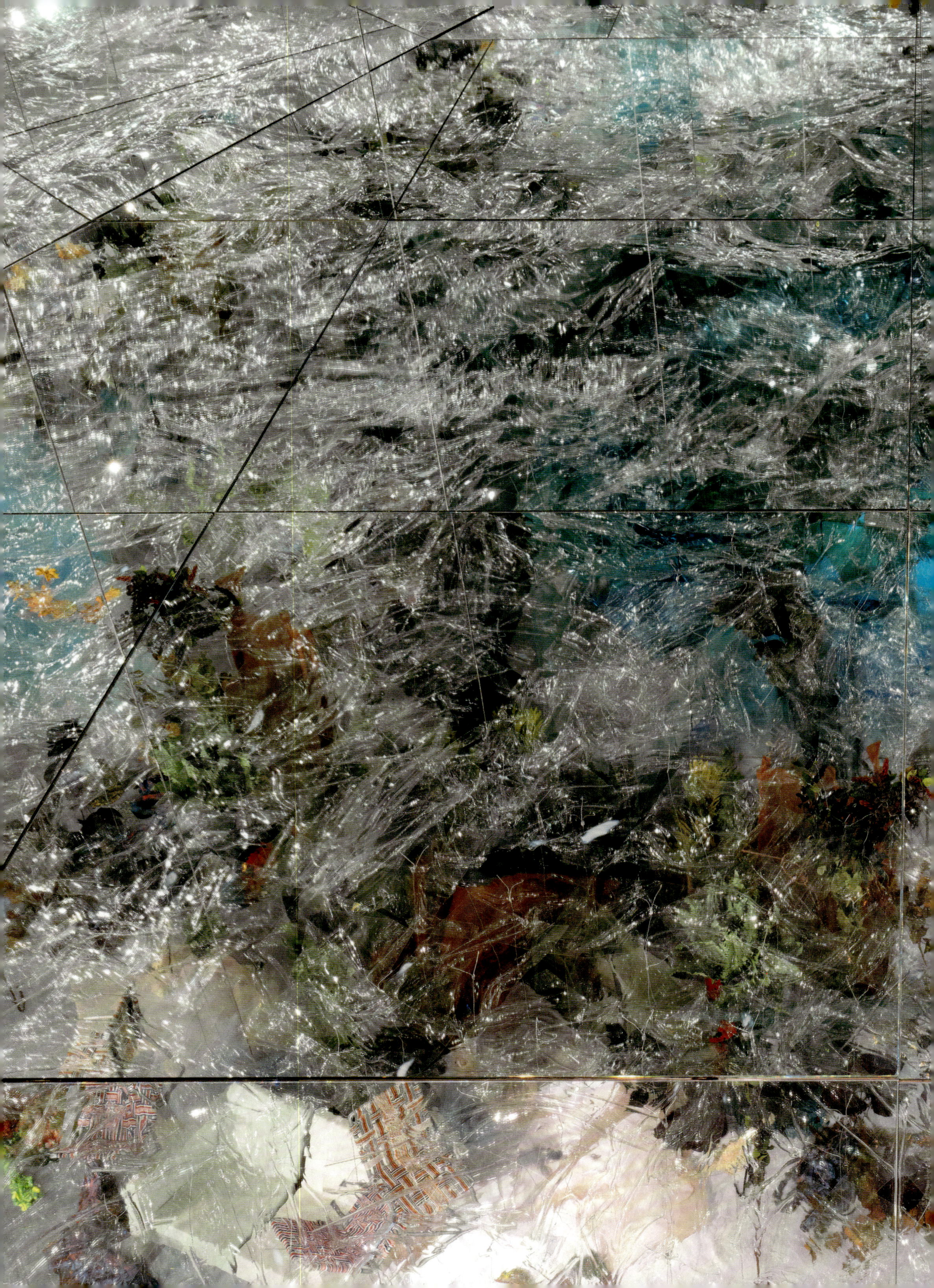

In Golden's early installations, video was often an important component. In *The Fireplace* (2013), closed-circuit feedback footage placed images of visitors within the artwork. The inclusion of reflective surfaces there and in *Rape of the Mirror* (2011; FIG. 2) and *Mass Murder* (2014; FIG. 3) eventually yielded entire spaces generated by Golden's skillful deployment of mirrors within architectural settings to create what she has described as a kind of mental metaphor for complex levels of meaning.[7] In *The Flat Side*

FIG. 2. Samara Golden, *Rape of the Mirror*, 2011.
Foam insulation board, mirror, monitors, carpet,
projection, and other materials

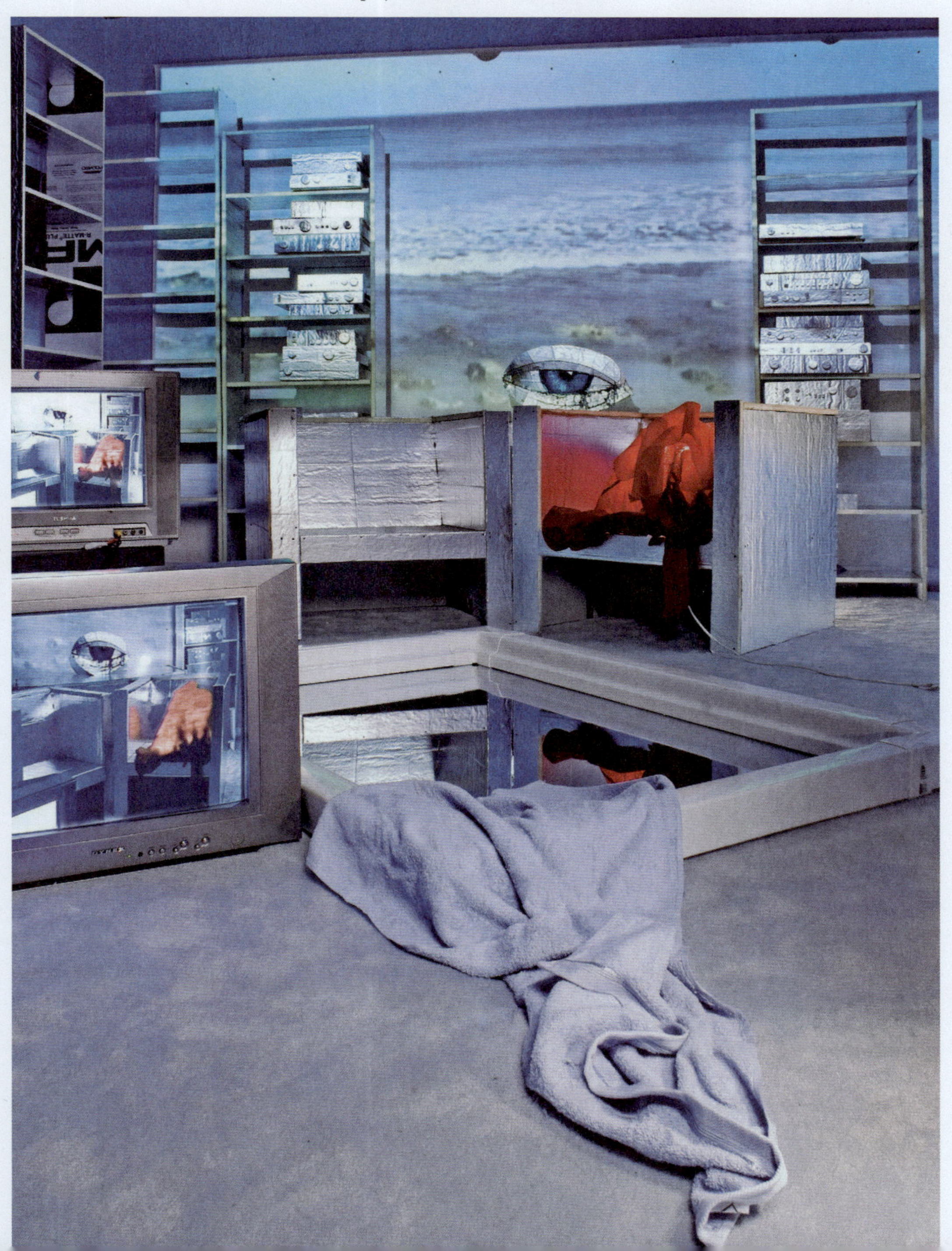

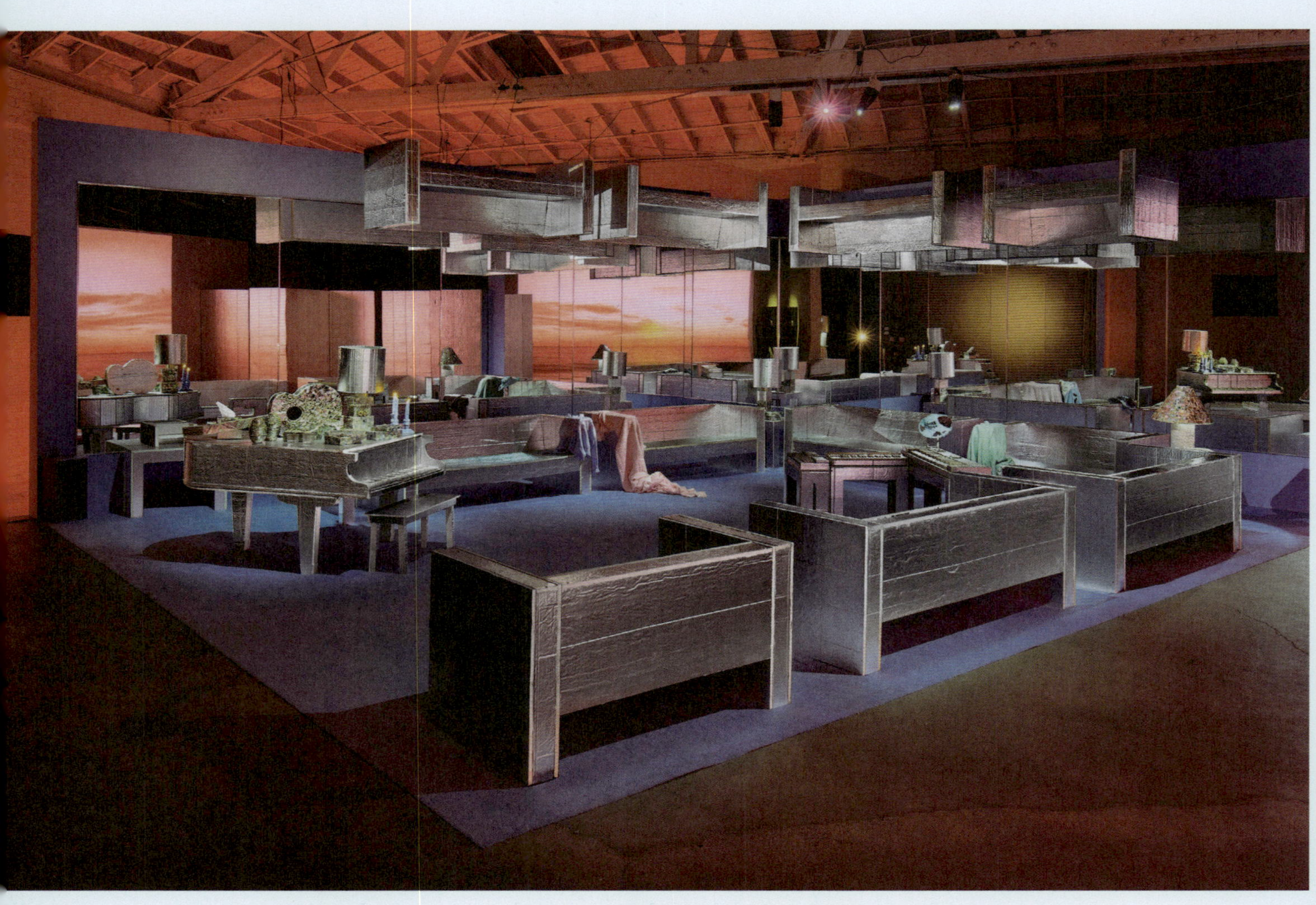

FIG. 3. Samara Golden, *Mass Murder*, 2014.
Foam insulation board, mirror, video projection,
carpet, and other materials

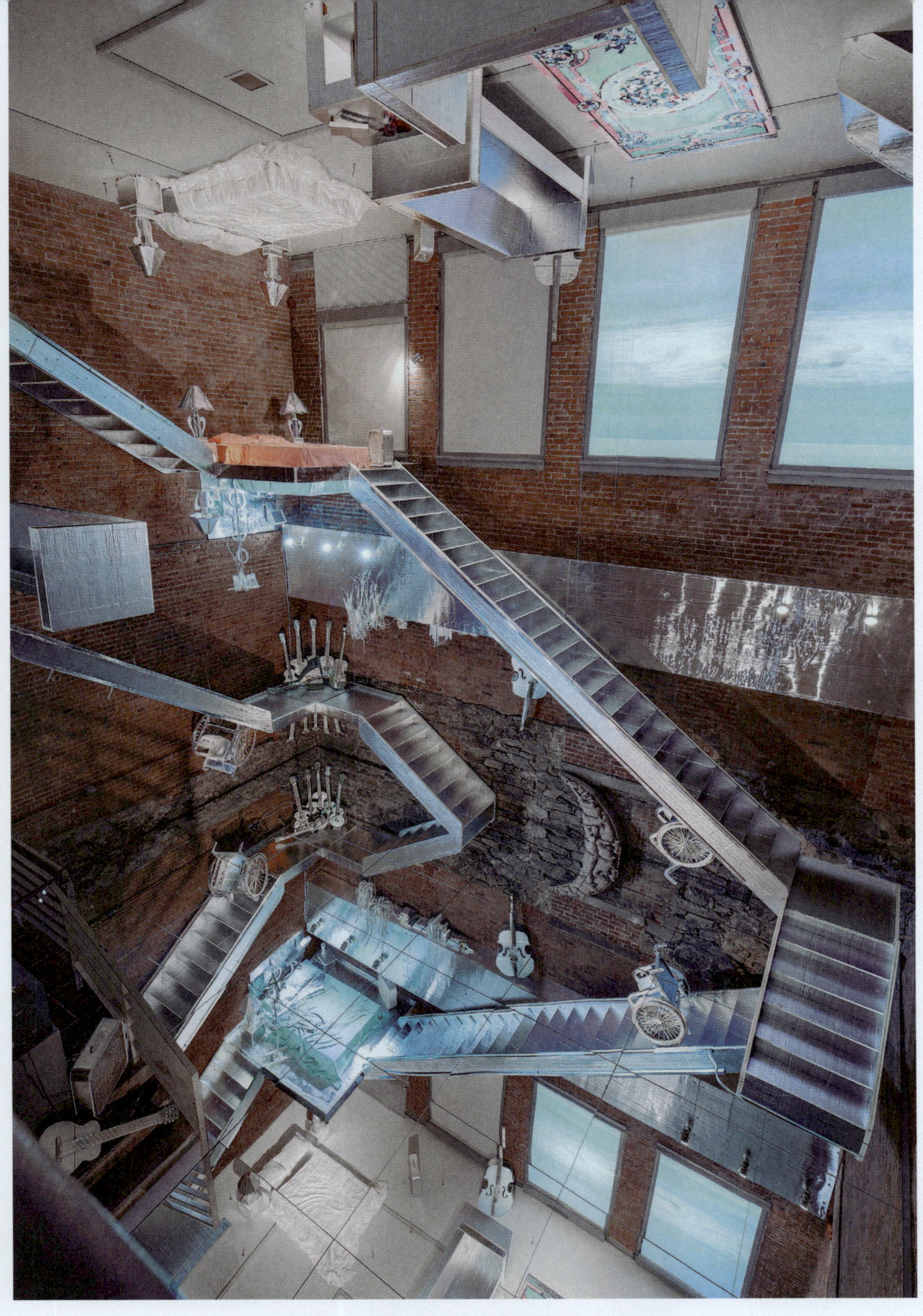

FIG. 4. Samara Golden, *The Flat Side of the Knife*, 2014.
Foam insulation board, mirror, monitors,
video projection, carpet, sound, and other materials

of the Knife (2014; FIG. 4) at MoMA PS1, New York, these layers evoked both a hospital room filled with medical equipment and a sunny beach house. For *The Meat Grinder's Iron Clothes* (FIG. 5), her monumental contribution to the 2017 Whitney Biennial, Golden multiplied these strata to conjure the anxieties of class insecurity. A serenely appointed apartment appeared at the top in a vision of the American dream as aspirational wealth; descending levels showed spaces suggesting a hotel workout room; Golden's own apartment and the houses she grew up in; and finally a community clinic and shelter, with small figures that appeared to be sleeping on distant heating grates—those left behind, or fallen, on the way up to the penthouse.

As with her Nasher installation, in these and other works Golden created viewing platforms for spectators, holding them at bay while offering a shared position of communal viewing. For *Upstairs at Steve's* (2020; FIG. 6) at Philadelphia's Fabric Workshop and Museum, Golden designed a space centered on the large windows at one end of the gallery. Multiplied by mirrors, the windows became the façade of a lighthouse positioned in the midst of dunes

FIG. 5. Samara Golden, *The Meat Grinder's Iron Clothes*, 2017.
Insulation foamboard, extruded polystyrene,
epoxy resin, carpet, vinyl, fabric, acrylic paint, spray paint,
nail polish, plastic, altered found objects, and mirror

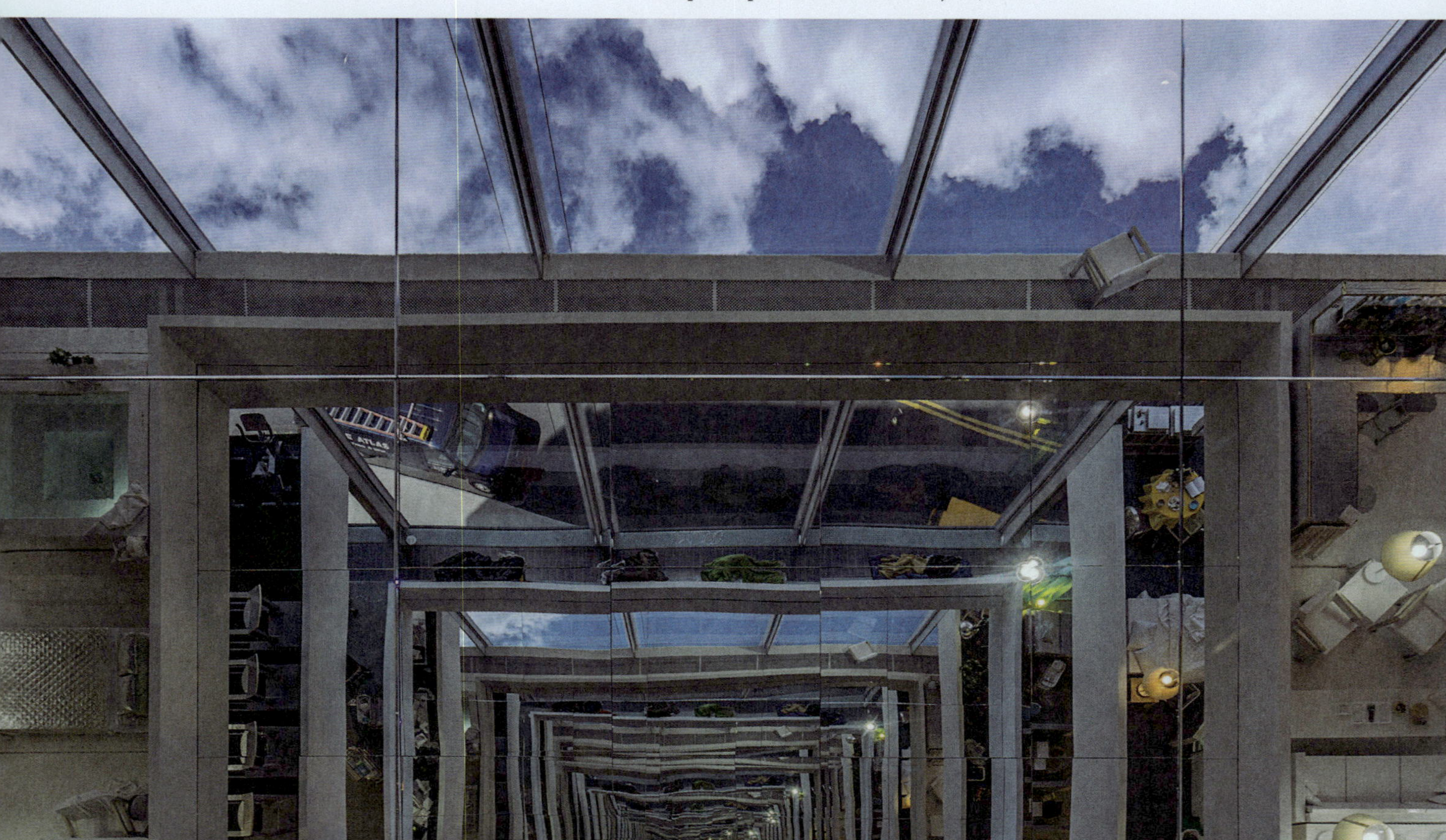

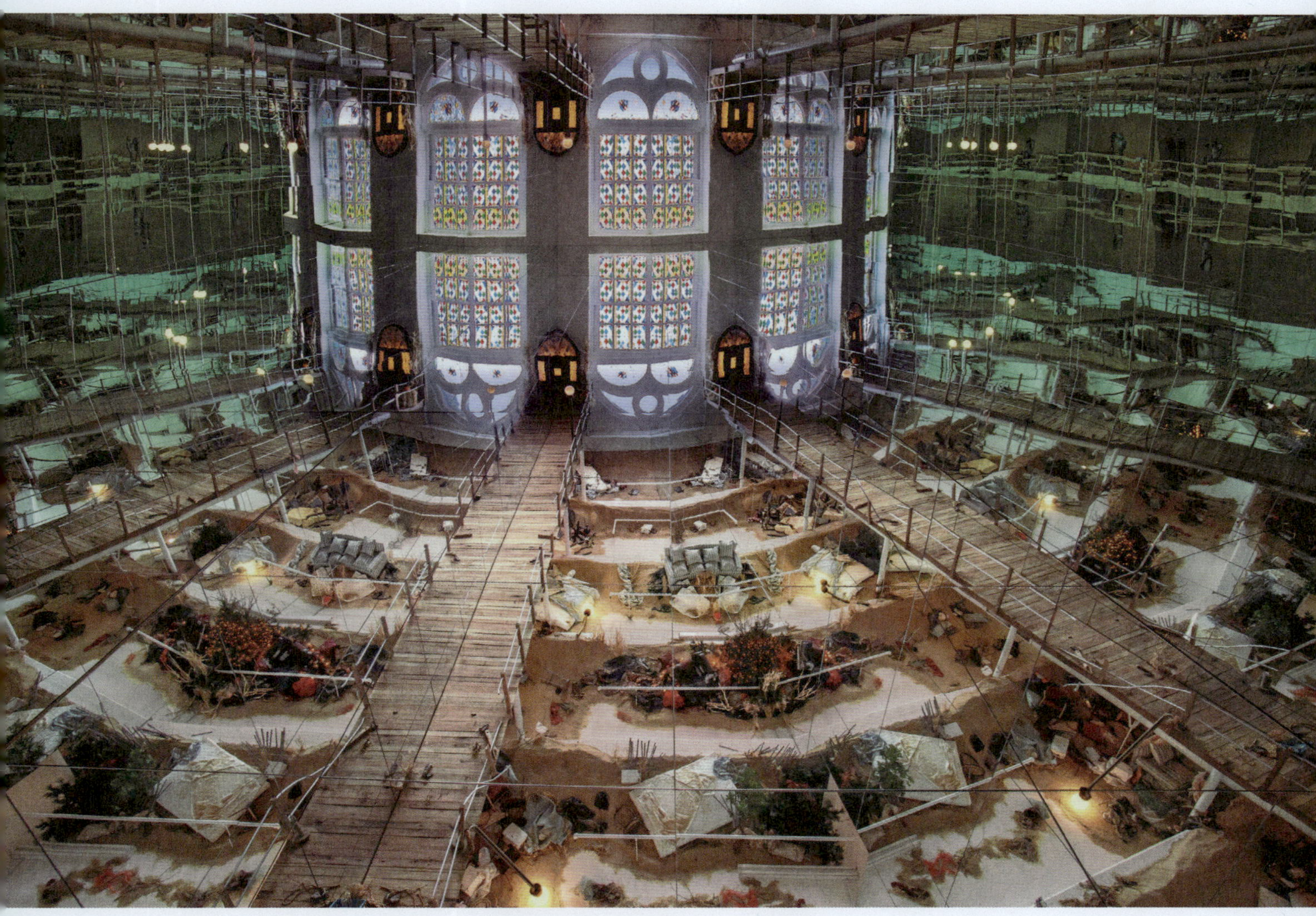

FIG. 6. Samara Golden, *Upstairs at Steve's*, 2020.
Mixed media

bridged by boardwalks constructed over heaps of sand containing a disturbing range of debris, as if from some catastrophic storm. A similar railing and platform was used for *Guts* (2022; FIG. 7), a piece also marking a significant point of departure within the artist's familiar framework of the multilevel architectural form, which in this case resembled the atrium of a skyscraper.[8] Each level was not only decidedly distinct but also contained things that could never be found in a building: the seething title element, painted in

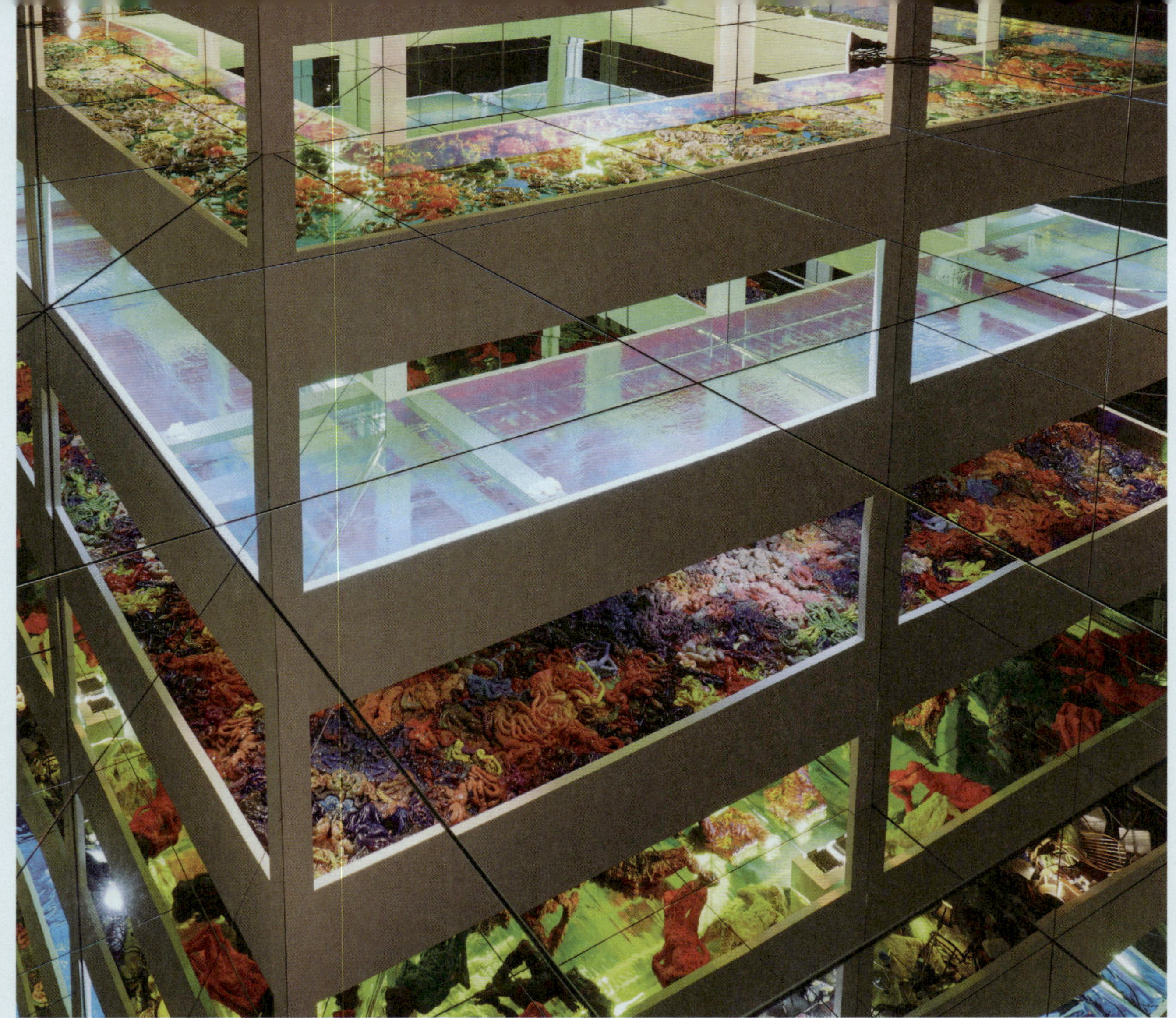

a vibrant if slightly queasy array of colors; multihued snakes and crabs; similarly painted human figures; and a jumble of furniture. Interspersed with these scenes were floors covered with expanses of a rich, calm blue, created with shimmering dichroic vinyl, a material that appears to fluidly shift color depending on the light.

Golden has never been interested in manipulating mirrors to make illusionistic environments that fool the eye. Instead, she has sought to create spaces that can't exist and can't be explained, prompting questions that may have no answers. Mirrors, she had realized, offered the best way to foster these sensations: "In *Mass Murder* . . . it became clear during construction that what was happening in the mirror was actually the whole point of the piece. And everything creating the reflections, everything I painstakingly built, was in service to this thing happening inside the mirror."[9]

Often, these spaces have been sites of concern, illness, trauma, and recovery, prompting responses from viewers that can encompass uneasiness or anxiety. Especially in her earlier works, Golden drew on her past to inspire specific environments, such as her grandparents' homes in *Mass Murder* and her experience of severe illness following a tonsillectomy for the hospital room of *The Flat Side of the Knife* (FIG. 8). On several occasions, she has attempted to give physical form to the flickering optical phenomena produced

FIG. 8. Samara Golden, *The Flat Side of the Knife* (detail with hospital bed), 2014

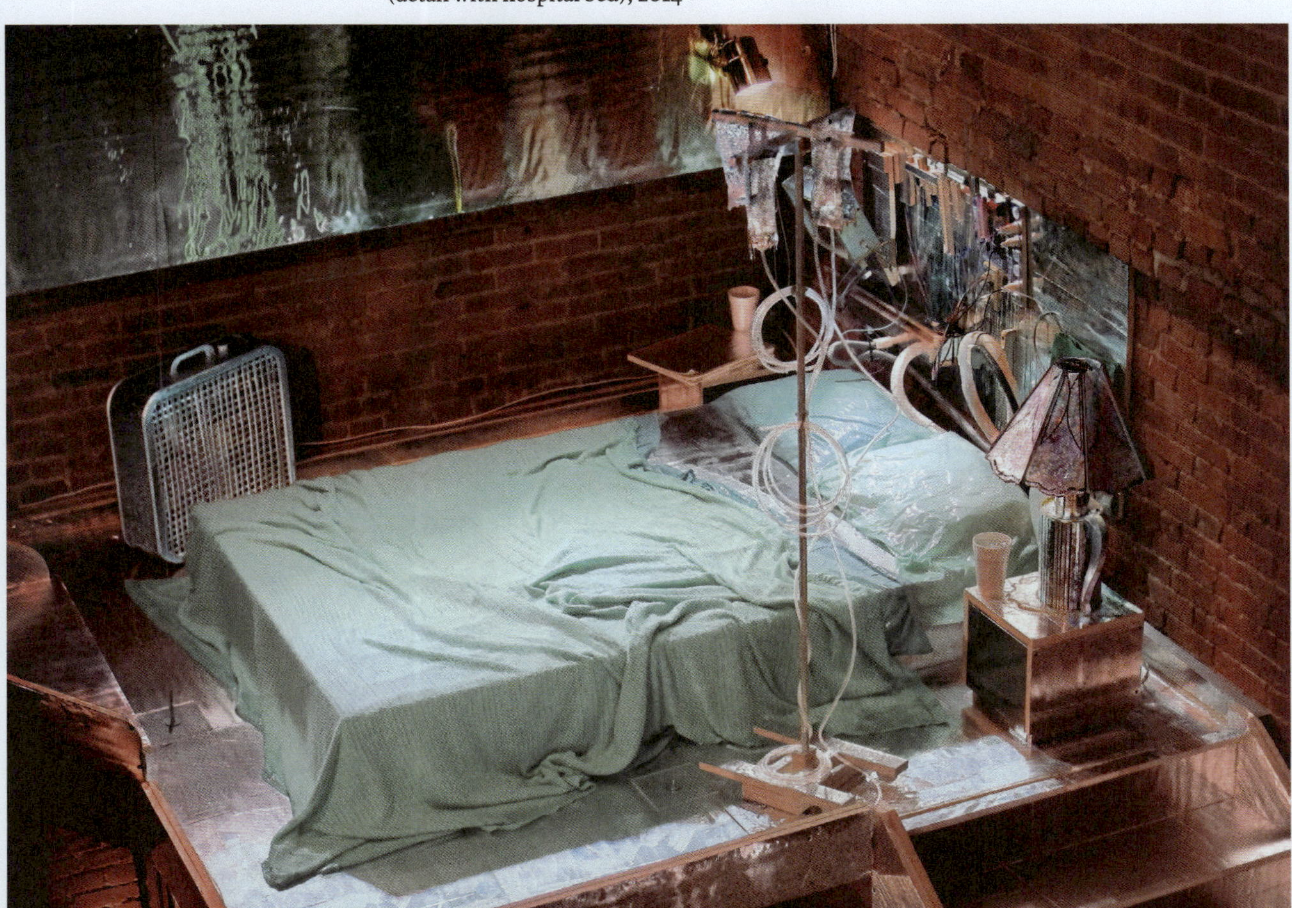

when she suffers migraines, and to the small animals she witnessed during a bout of fever hallucinations after her tonsillectomy, as seen in *The Fireplace*, *Mass Murder*, and *The Flat Side of the Knife*.

Likewise, her interest in class distinctions also has traces in her personal history. Golden had what she has described as an unconventional upbringing.[10] On several occasions, her father, a photographer, took her as an assistant on an assignment to shoot interiors of nursing homes in the American South. Before taking photographs, the rooms and common areas needed to be made more presentable and cheerful, with such additions as flowers; Golden was struck by the discrepancy of the marketing image and the lonely reality of the residents' daily existence. Years later, as a young woman, she spent time riding the rails across the country, an experience that left her with a lasting identification with those who are unhoused or otherwise invisible to much of society.[11]

Creating environments real enough in their materiality to provoke an engaged response has long been an exacting process for Golden. Determining the size of the space, the angles of the mirrors, and the placement of sculptures can be daunting. Yet discoveries made during the uncertain periods of creation and installation are also crucial to her practice. This give-and-take has prompted her in recent years to attempt relinquishing some control, leaving, for example, more of the placement of sculptural elements to improvisation during a piece's installation, as she did at the Nasher. At the same time she has expanded her subject matter. Indeed, the epic scale of *The Meat Grinder's Iron Clothes* seems to signal the culmination of one chapter of her work, linked to the urban or suburban environment and Golden's own past and medical trauma.

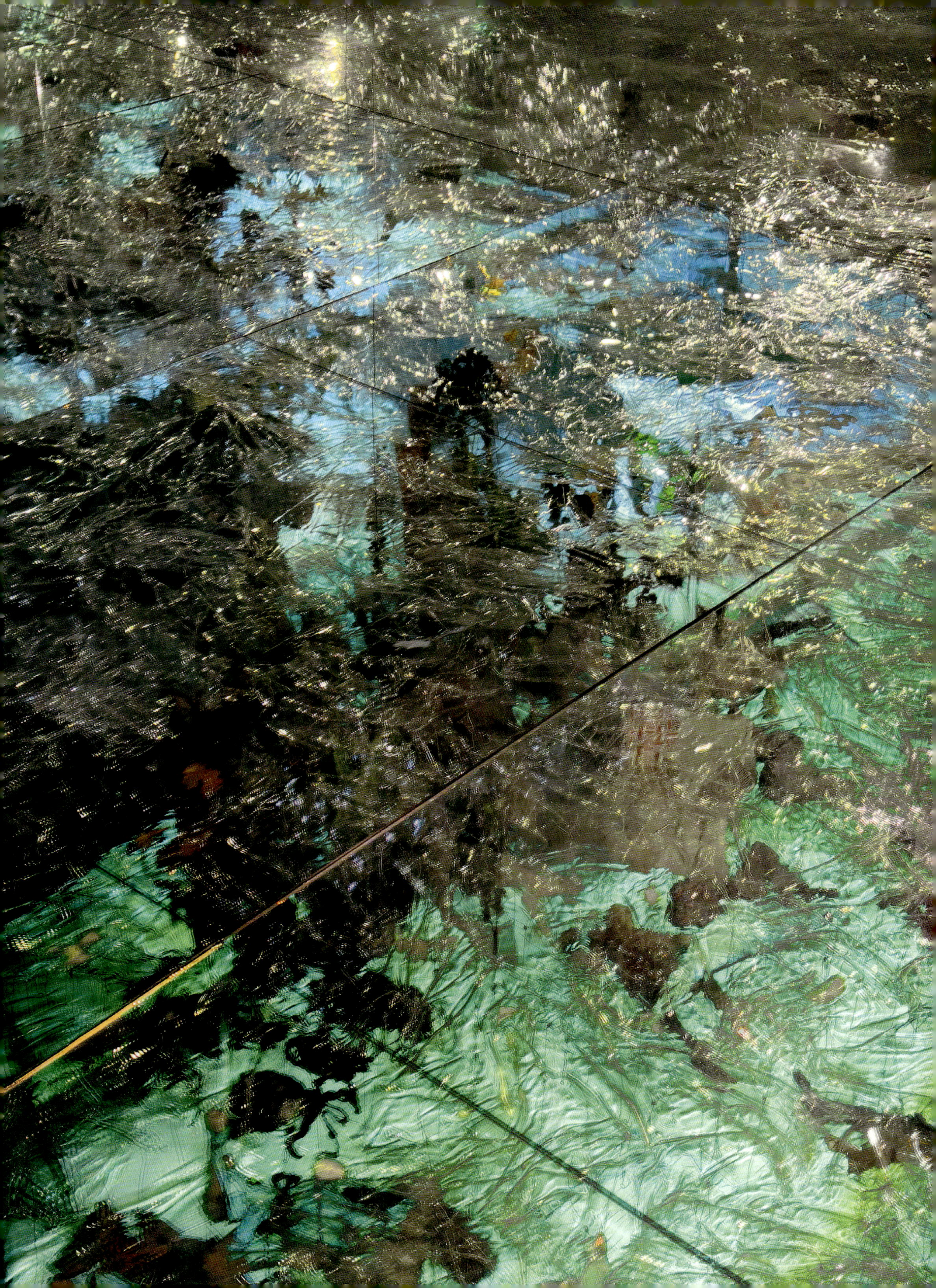

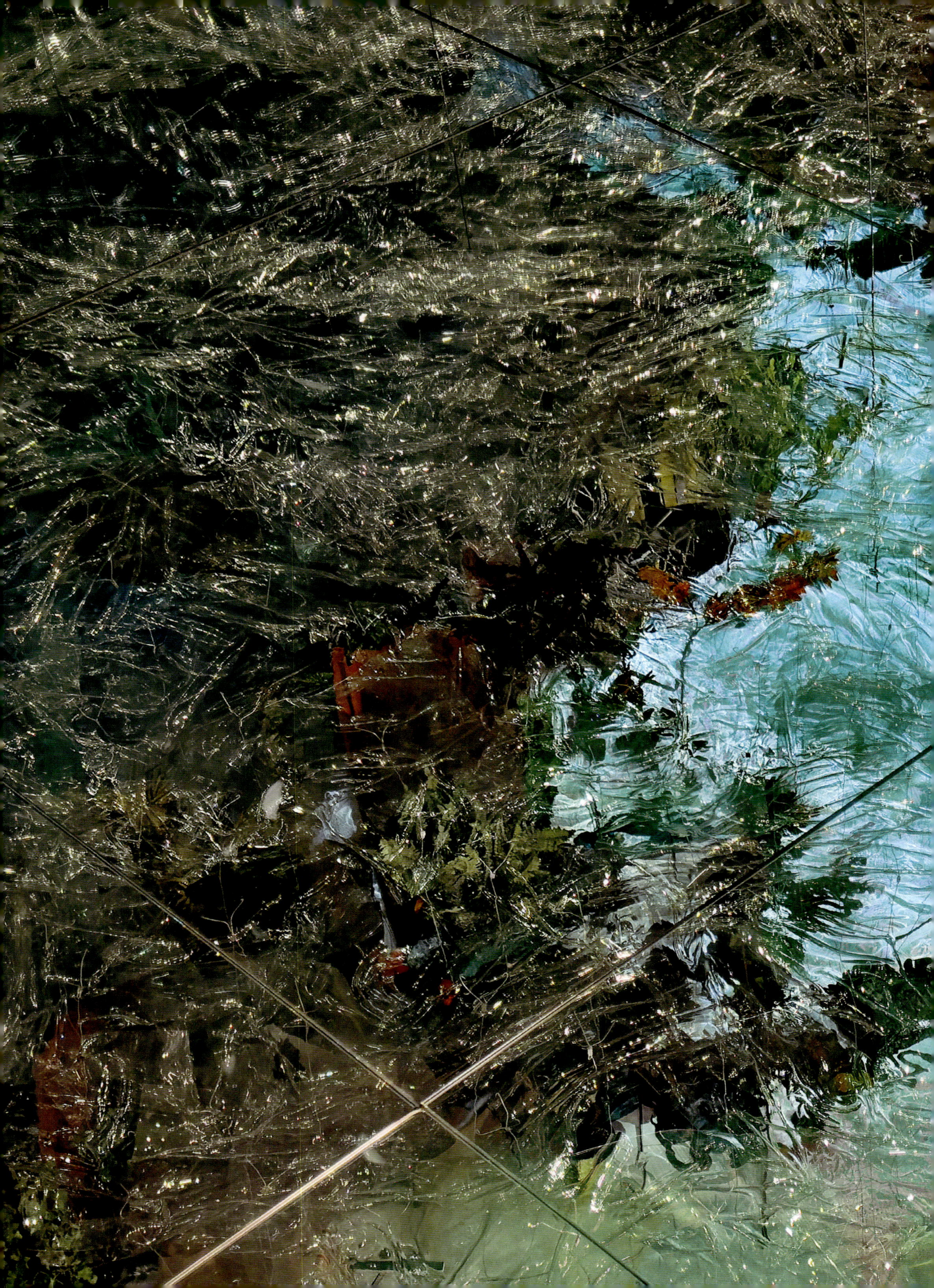

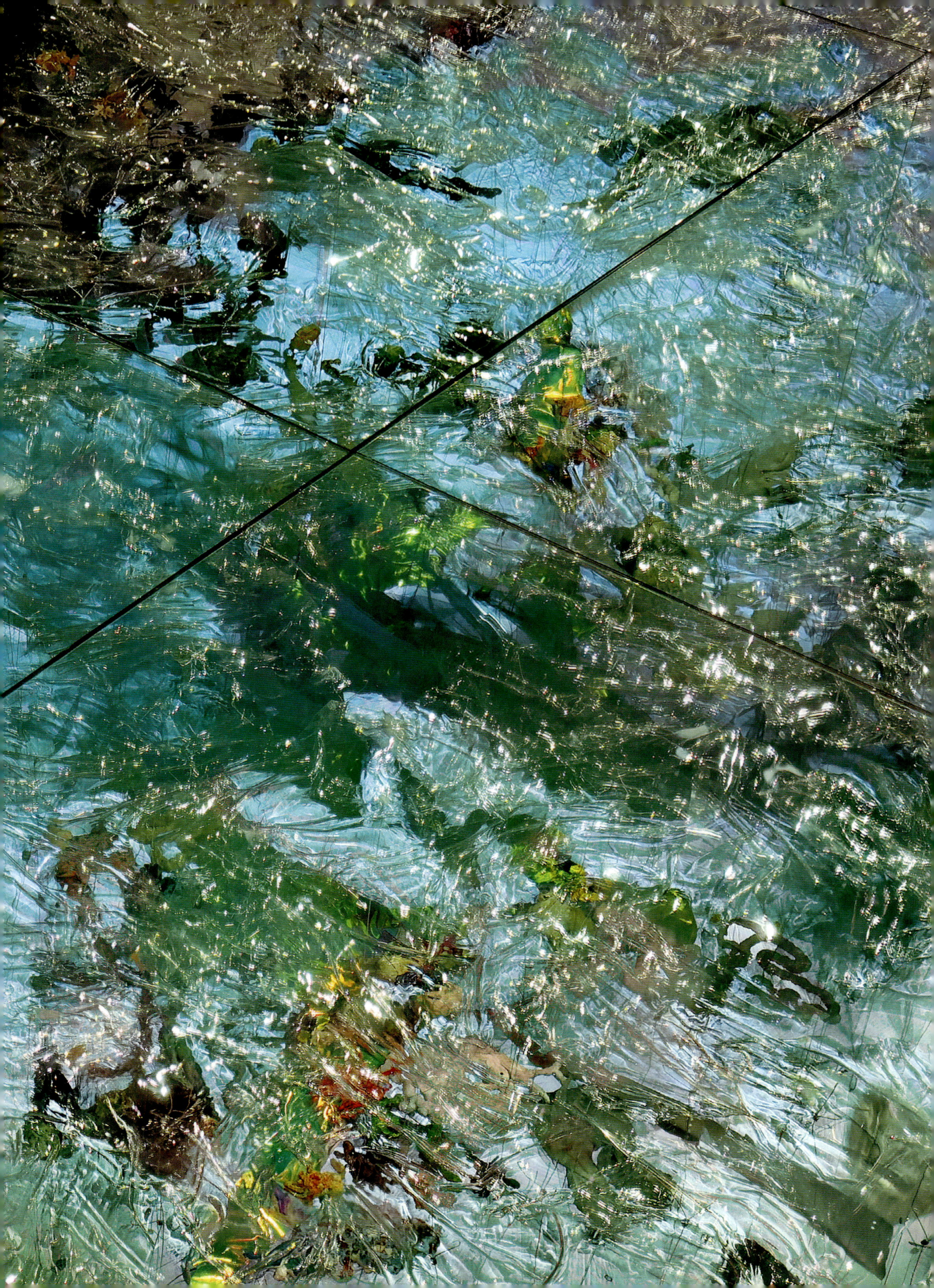

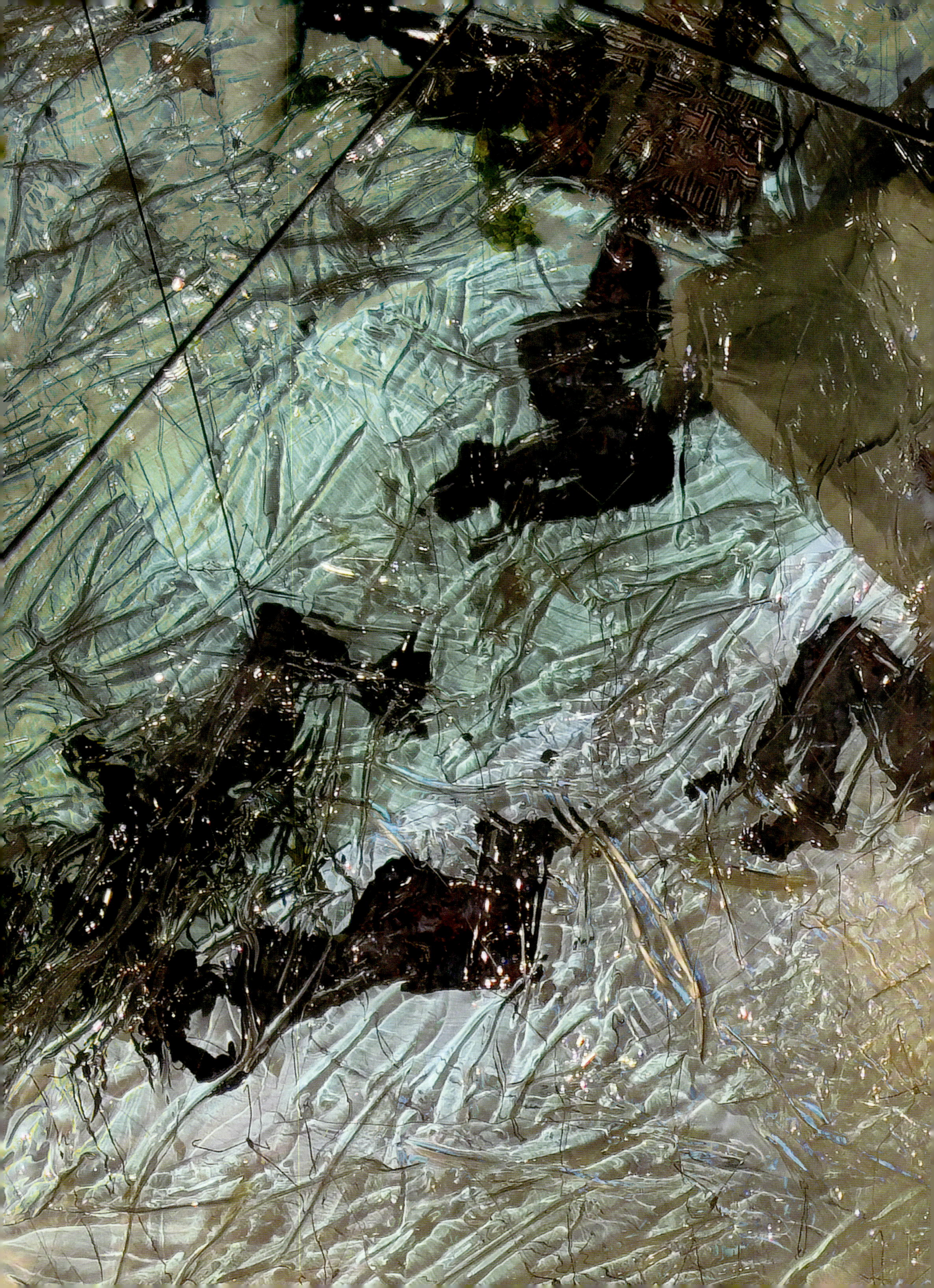

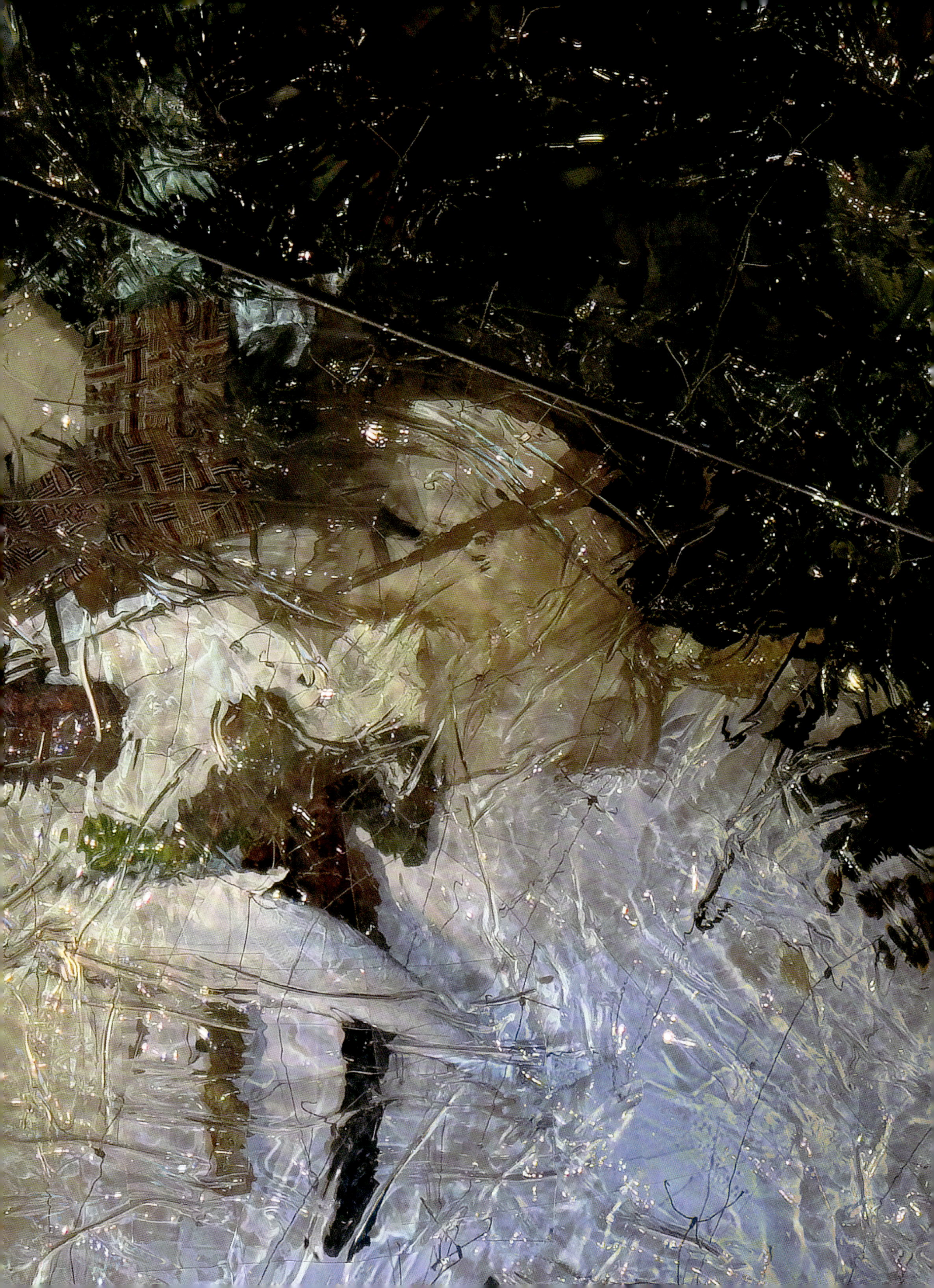

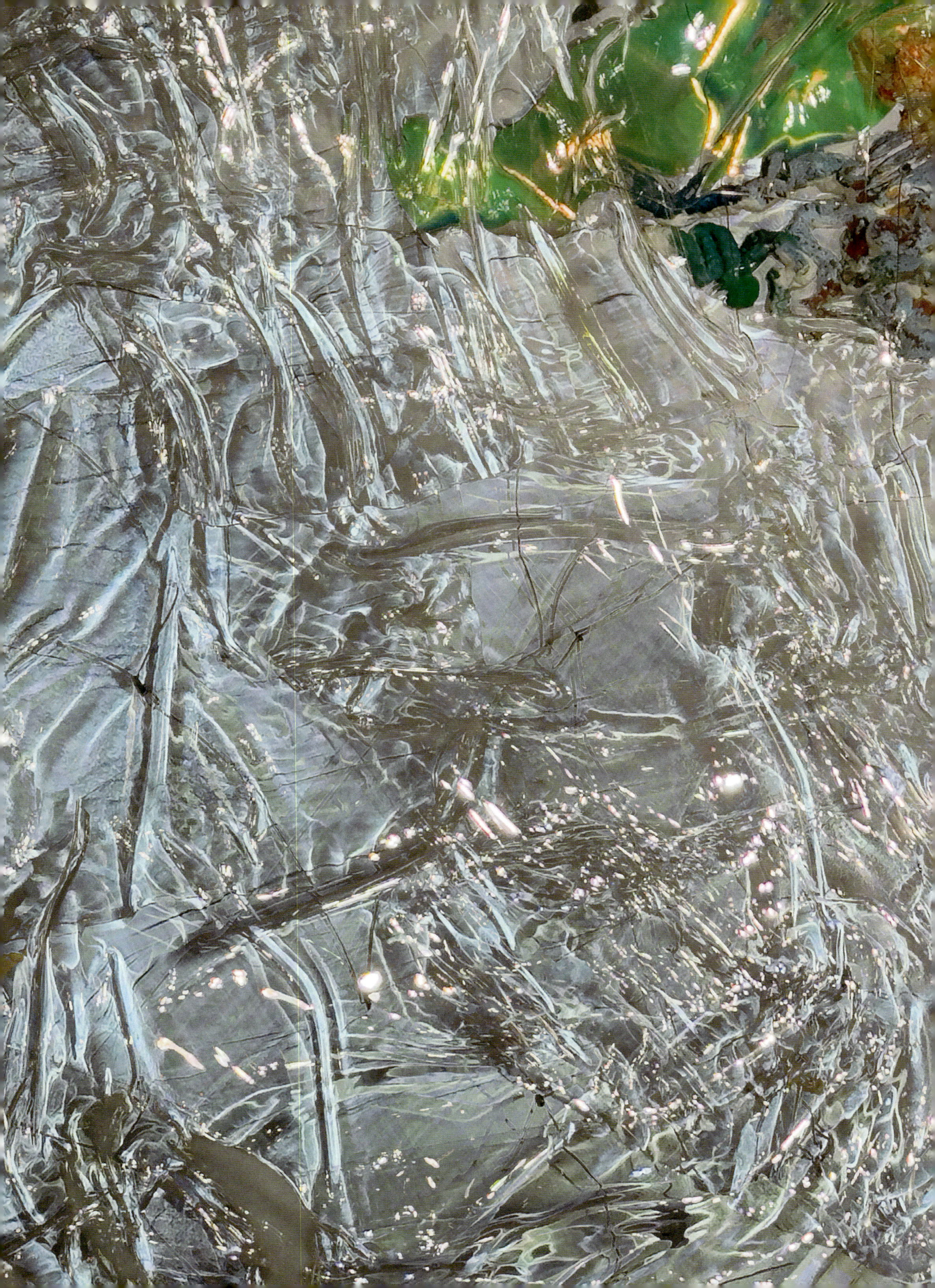

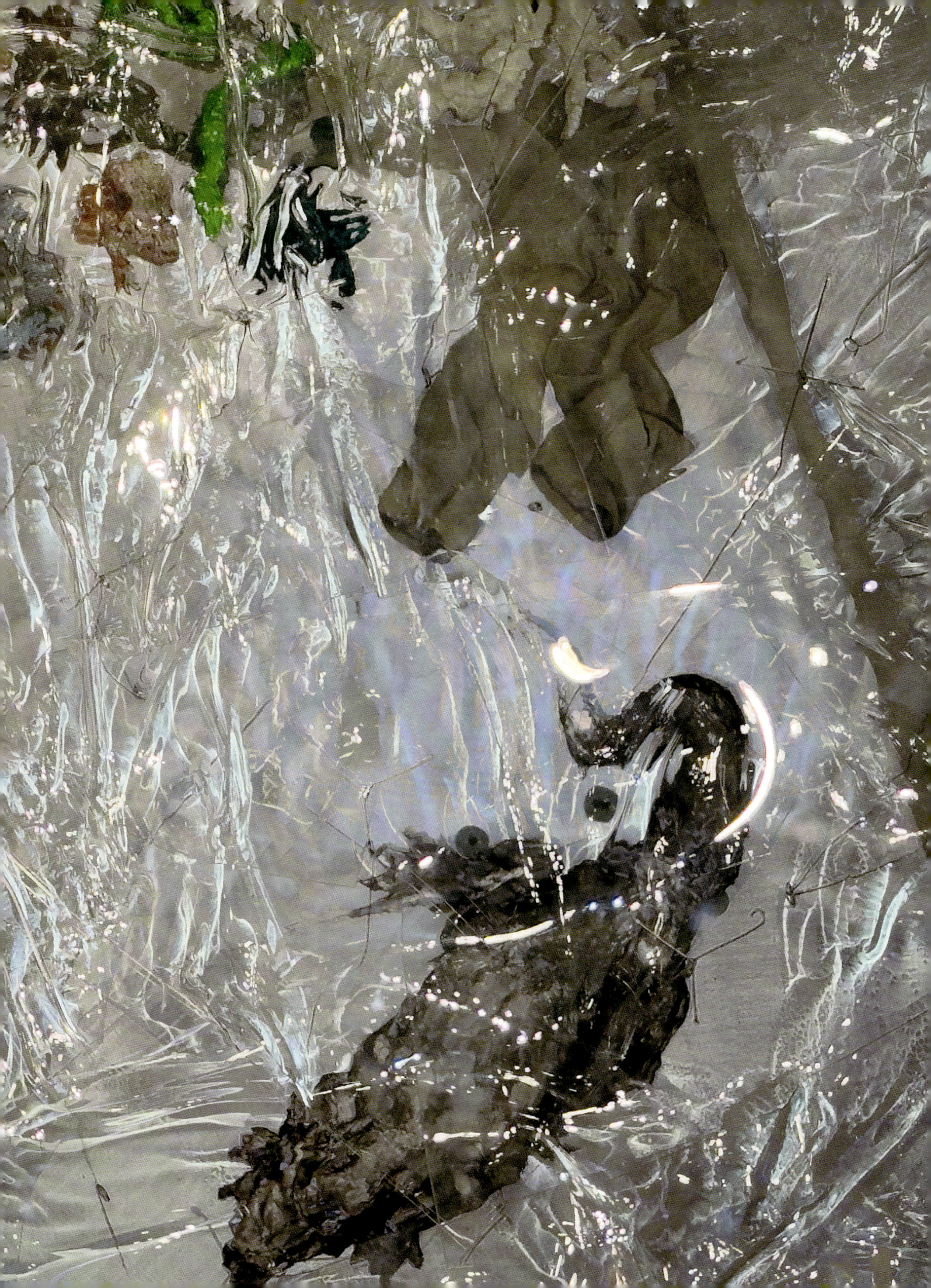

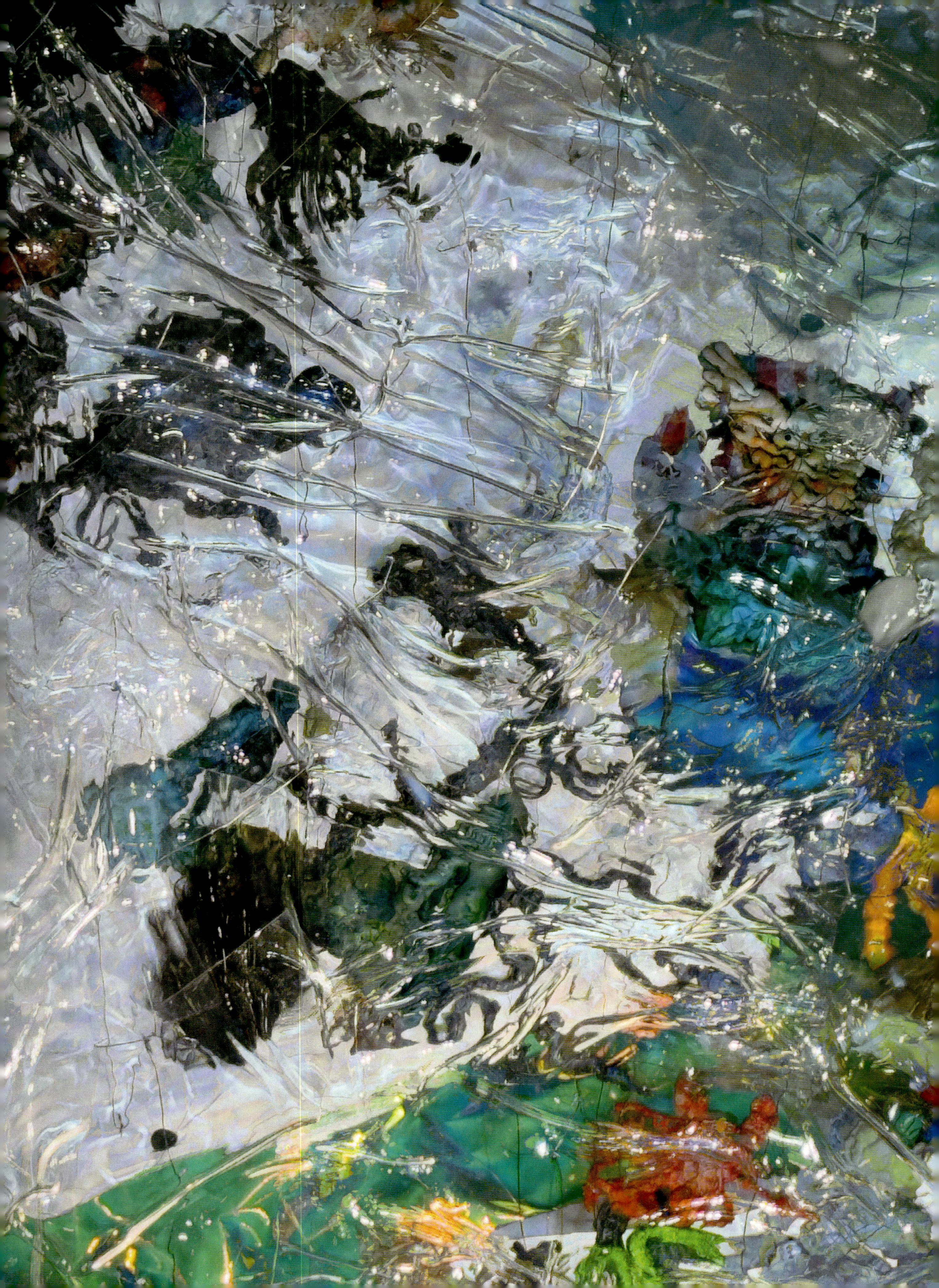

Upstairs at Steve's is somewhat transitional in this regard, prompted by both the opportunity of a residency at the Fabric Workshop and the death of Golden's brother-in-law as a result of amyotrophic lateral sclerosis (ALS), a progressive neurodegenerative disease. In Philadelphia, Golden found a team of assistants and preparators ready to help her produce the small sculptural objects that would go into the installation, an unusual situation for an artist who typically makes everything herself. Their research also increased her familiarity with dichroic and reflective fabrics. The fantastical installation that resulted took its cue, on the one hand, from a beloved album of Golden's youth, Yaz's *Upstairs at Eric's* (1982). Shifting the artwork's title to the name of her brother-in-law yielded a metaphor for the toll of the disease, as ALS typically wreaks havoc on the body while leaving the mind intact. *Upstairs at Steve's* plays upon the incommunicable interiority of being in the head of someone who cannot tell you how he is feeling, an isolation that can only be witnessed, from a distance.

Only weeks before *Upstairs at Steve's* was to open, the Covid-19 pandemic required the closure of the Fabric Workshop, pushing the exhibition opening back to September 2020. Her next undertaking, *Guts*, was commissioned by the Art Gallery of New South Wales in Sydney, Australia, and drew on her experience of the isolation and stress of the pandemic. *Guts* plays on the multiple meanings held by the title: one's internal organs and their myriad vulnerabilities; the pull of intuition; and the grit and courage to act. The title offers options echoed in the strata of the work, which Golden has described as "different ways of being in the world."[12]

Just below the level with the eponymous viscera of the title is another filled with human figures, likewise made with spray insulation foam and painted in colors as lurid as those of the piece's entrails and sea life (FIG. 9). The figures seem to recline, swim, or writhe in a yellow-orange glow, suggesting both the warmth of the sun as well as a more infernal source of heat. If their state is ambiguous, the figures populating a slightly earlier installation appear less so. In 2019,

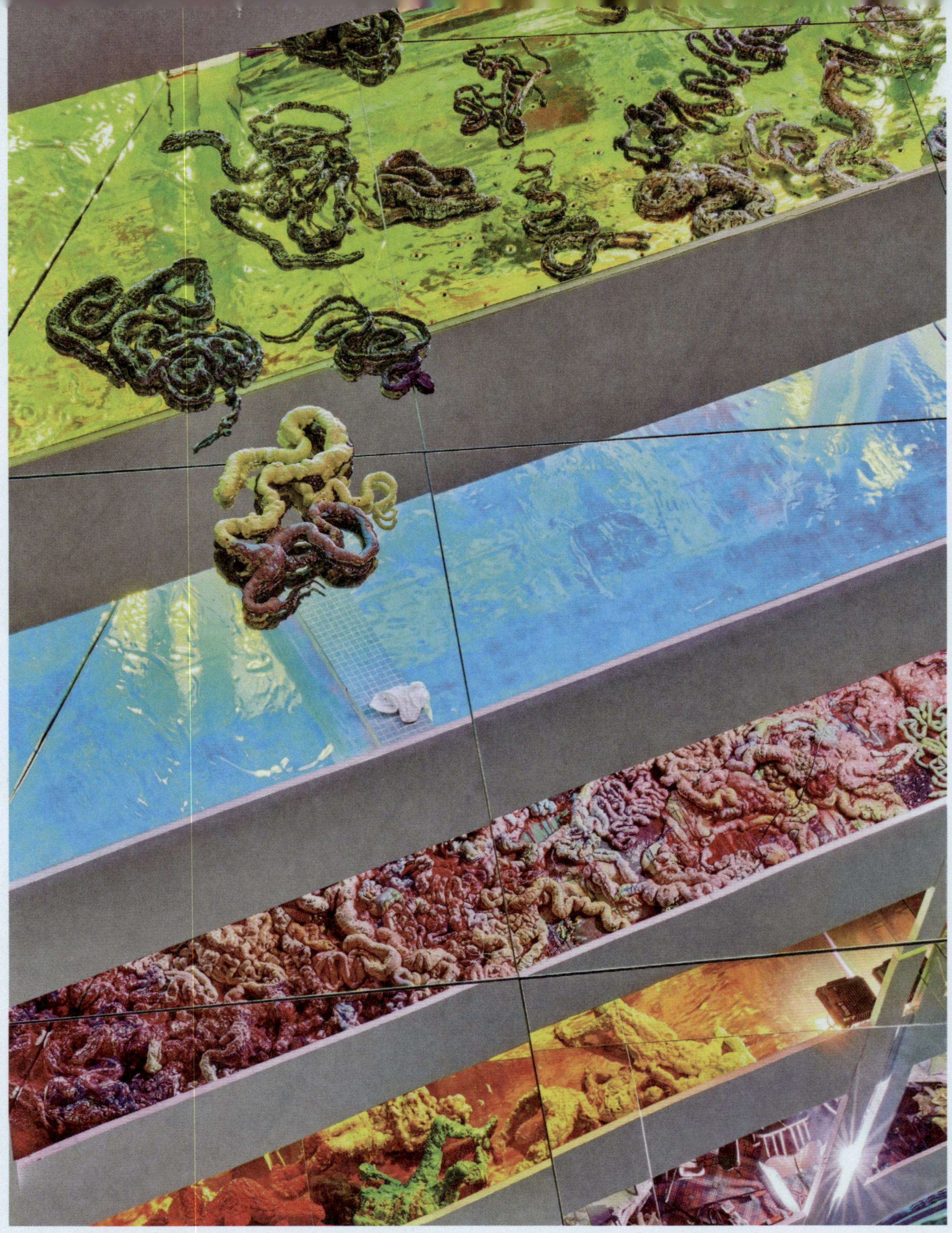

FIG. 9. Samara Golden, *Guts* (detail), 2022

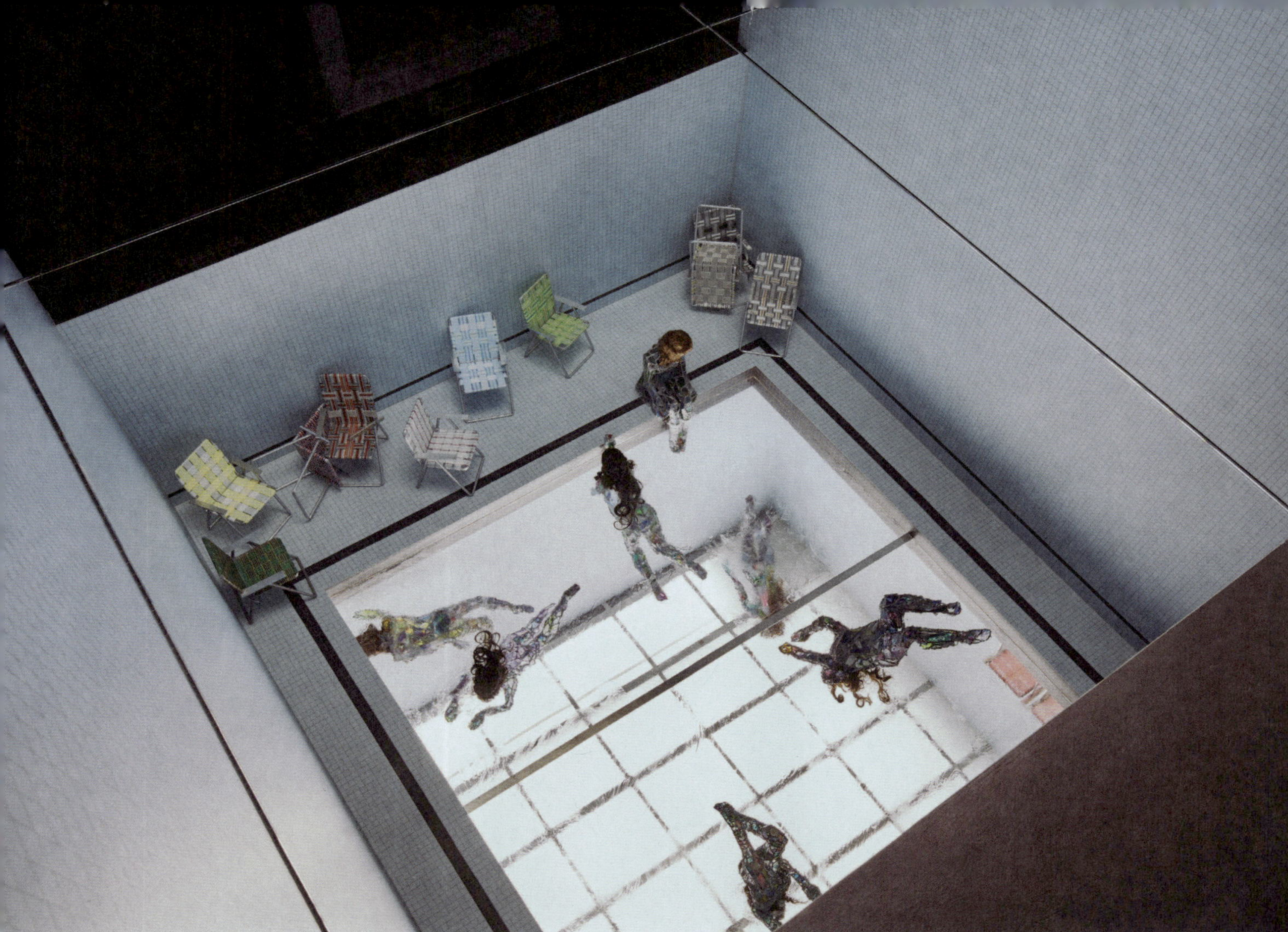

FIG. 10. Samara Golden,
The Lamplighter's Wooden Pajamas, 2019.
Mixed media

the Kunsthalle Baden-Baden hosted the group exhibition *Psyche and Politics*, for which Golden created *The Lamplighter's Wooden Pajamas*, an installation including similar figures (FIG. 10). There she sited the work in a small gallery with a skylight, and—as at the Nasher—she did not place mirrors on the ceiling. Instead, visitors looking down at the mirrored floor would see reflected back the appearance of great depth, with figures suspended so that they seemed to be floating or swimming; one figure sat at the edge of the skylight, which became a pool containing the other swimmers. It seemed idyllic, a moment of calm, stillness, and mutual care in an impossible place.

FIG. 11. Samara Golden, *The Fireplace* (detail), 2013. Mixed media

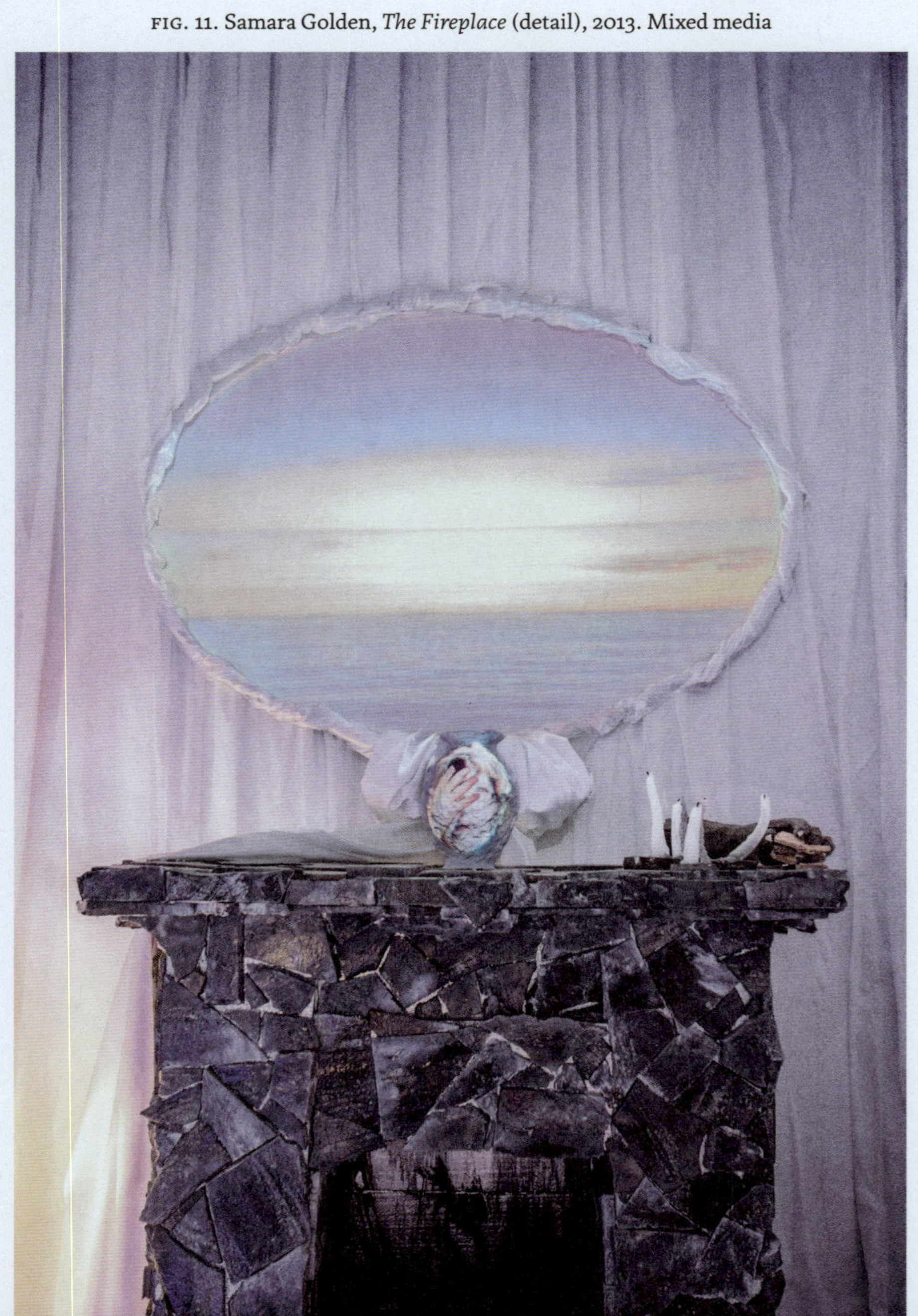

The Nasher piece marks the first time Golden has challenged herself to create a large environment free of the layered architectural structures that have previously defined her practice. Turning to water, she focused on an element that has been a throughline of her art. One of her earliest documented works, *"Curator Howardina D'Ville Visits Artist Samara Golden at her Los Angeles"* [sic] (2009), features a "carved hot dog person" lounging in a miniature hot tub and may be a reference to Golden's then-recent move to Los Angeles from New York, where she had just received her MFA from Columbia University. In fact, her interest in Los Angeles stemmed in part from its cultural associations with the ocean, the beach, and the good life that the city seemed to promise, as prominently featured in Hollywood movies and television shows. In the concatenation of images that flash by on the video screen of another early work, *The Fireplace* (FIG. 11), can be glimpsed a peaceful seascape; a sunset over the ocean is a prominent element in both *Rape of the Mirror* and *The Flat Side of the Knife*, which includes the sound of ocean waves on its soundtrack. Images of water and its reflections likewise animate parts of *Bad Brains* (2012) and *Mass Murder*, and the dreamlike world of *The Meat Grinder's New Clothes* includes a miniature hot tub on one level.

In many of these earlier works, the presence of water suggests the mediated images of a TV program, but more recently, scenes implying the direct experience of water have proliferated. In *Upstairs at Steve's*, its proximity is strongly suggested just behind the lighthouse, through the drifts of sand beneath the boardwalk, and the detritus deposited by its unseen force. The lounge chairs and movements of swimming in *The Lamplighter's Wooden Pajamas* imply poolside relaxation, while two floors of *Guts* evoke, through their blue vinyl, a glittering expanse of calm water, with the crabs and snakes that may share, and hamper, enjoyment of the seaside mostly exiled to another level.

if earth is the brain then where is the body offered up the contradictory spectacle of an expansive body of water that appears to have a handrail running all the way around it in a space that could not possibly contain it. Gazing straight down, visitors saw a range of creatures underwater, including dolphins, sharks, and crabs; when directly lit, the reflective gray fabric cladding the ceiling paled to the brightness of white sand. That some of these creatures, such as alligators and snakes, cannot actually live underwater was one of the first challenges to the scene's realism. No matter: the water made its own reality, which conducted itself according to its own rules. Human figures were underwater, but some did not appear to be swimming. Two curled up on the water's floor while another rested in a static posture, arms outstretched. At right, large swaths of tulle suggested stretches of seaweed, while clumps of artificial plants, leaves, and flowers darkened the left side in an area Golden referred to as "swill." In the center, the water appeared to grow deeper, lit from far below by an eerie blue-green light.

To be sure, part of the inspiration for her body of water came from common images of relaxation and enjoyment—the serene, gentle waves of a tropical beach or the deep clear waters of lakes familiar from her upbringing in Michigan. But crashing into these visions was the reality that, along with many others, Golden is actually rather frightened of open water, especially the violent waves and insidious currents that can make swimming hazardous. Likewise, one of the inspirations for the Nasher piece came during a visit to the Doge's Palace during a trip to Venice:

> [There] are paintings on the ceilings with things like battle scenes. In the corners there are fish and clams intertwined in dark, swirling water. The same kind of murky mix of sea life, dirt, and seaweed is in the gutters around the city. I kept having dreams of swirling seaweed while I was there.[13]

As Golden's recollection indicates, along with the incipient threat of unrestrained nature came more emphatically human interferences. Fetid water can exist in nature, but often such bodies of water result from pollution, as suggested by Golden's associations of the "swill" with nuclear wastewater.[14] Human carelessness is further signaled by an abandoned loveseat and jumbles of folding chairs that have ended up in the water. Remnants of installations past, they here became refuse dumped when their usefulness had ended.

Although they are in reality attached to the ceiling, all these elements are glimpsed as reflections; understood as being underwater, they are occasionally obscured by it as well. Golden's determination to set the water moving through the deployment of lights and fans animated it in a variety of ways. Closer to the railing, the waves rippled and shuddered; fans blowing just above the level with the water created currents that stirred the tulle seaweed and a pile of broken folding chairs on the edge of the deepening blue-green water, the fractured back of one chair swaying hypnotically. Further out, ringing the edges of the water were small flashes of movement, initially registered in one's peripheral vision: distant oscillations of the fans transmuted into the intermittent twinkles of raindrops. At the installation's center—that is, toward the back of the wedge-shaped space where fans had difficulty penetrating—the movement slowed and almost halted. With the mysterious glow of its blue-green lighting, the heart of the water appeared to be frozen into unmoving ice, crazed with a network of cracks.

Describing an artwork that no longer exists is challenging but scarcely more so than putting words to a work of art at all. The Greeks gave a name, *ekphrasis*, to this practice, and those who attempt it may find that purely descriptive language can fall short. John Keats opens "Ode on a Grecian Urn" (1819) with a series of unanswerable questions about the figures that populate an ancient vase:

> What men or gods are these? What maidens loth?
> What mad pursuit? What struggle to escape?
> What pipes and timbrels? What wild ecstasy?[15]

Keats's poem cannot provide answers to these queries but instead proposes that "heard melodies are sweet, but those unheard are sweeter." He evokes both through his poetry, an apt medium for considering Golden's work. Regarding her art's mind-bending complexity, she has explained the appeal of containing multiple, sometimes contradictory details within a larger structure: "I love the idea of having the poem within a poem within a poem within a poem."[16] The condensation this language suggests is potent, especially considering that poetry can take many forms—elegies, odes, lyrics, blank verse, sonnets, haiku. All of them partake of a sharpened focus on aspects of life, feeling, and memory that would otherwise pass by. Golden's installation likewise created a place where recollections, emotions, and thoughts converged in possibilities encompassing the oceanic reaches of the subconscious; the sensation of floating, suspended, as if in utero; and the enclosing depths that elicit the terror of drowning. While forever falling short of conjuring the complex, lived experience of *if earth is the brain then where is the body*, the words and images comprising this book offer another site for the convening of reflections prompted by Golden's installation and some of the cultural, artistic, and sculptural associations it drew into itself.

intention

The flickering of what appeared to be raindrops around the periphery of *if earth is the brain then where is the body* emerged unexpectedly from Golden's adjustments to the lighting just before the exhibition's opening. By that point, she had been at the museum installing for close to three weeks. The raindrops' shimmer into existence was a moment of grace. She had not intended them and could not have known they were going to happen. In that moment, the piece took on a life without her.

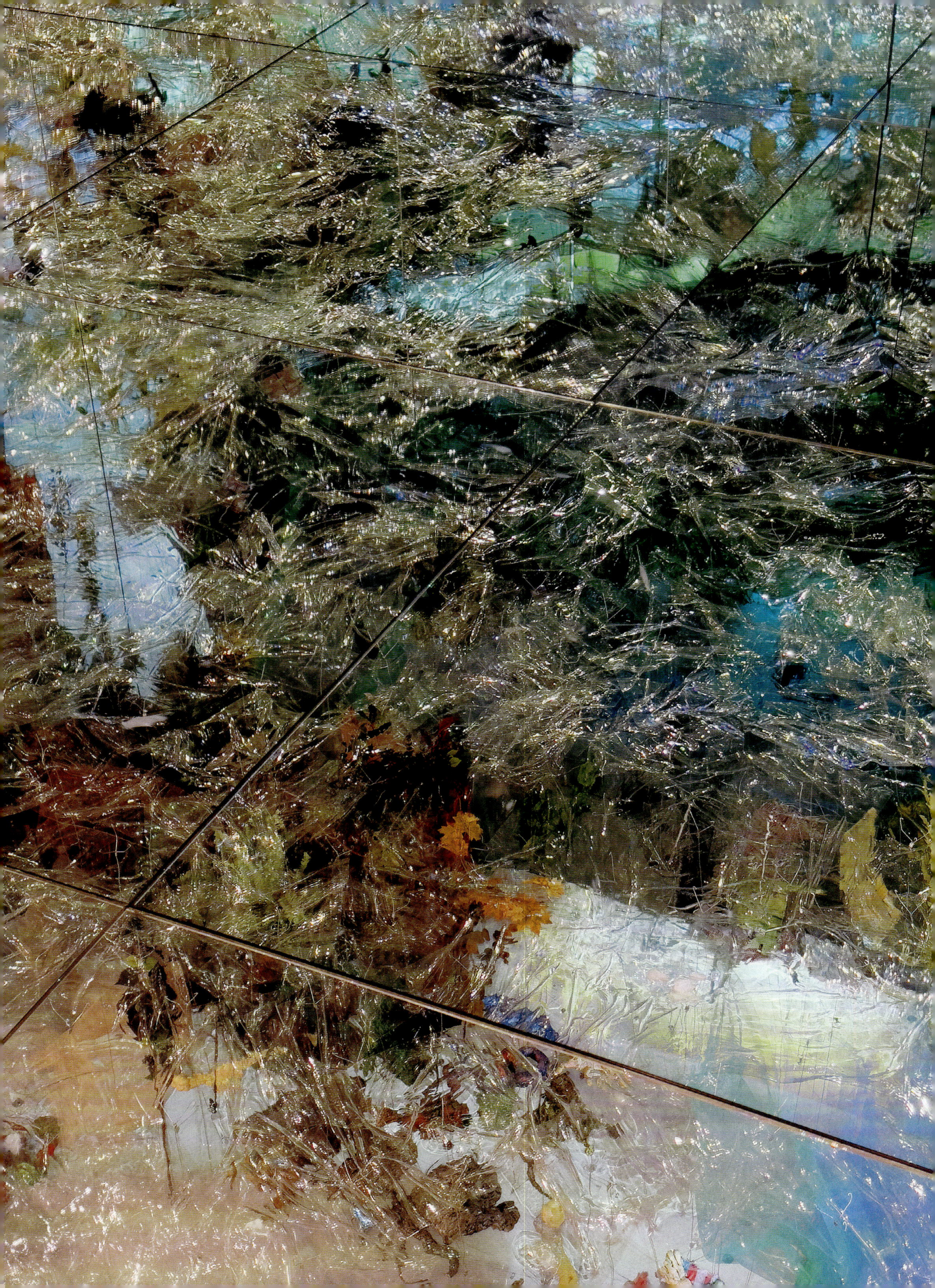

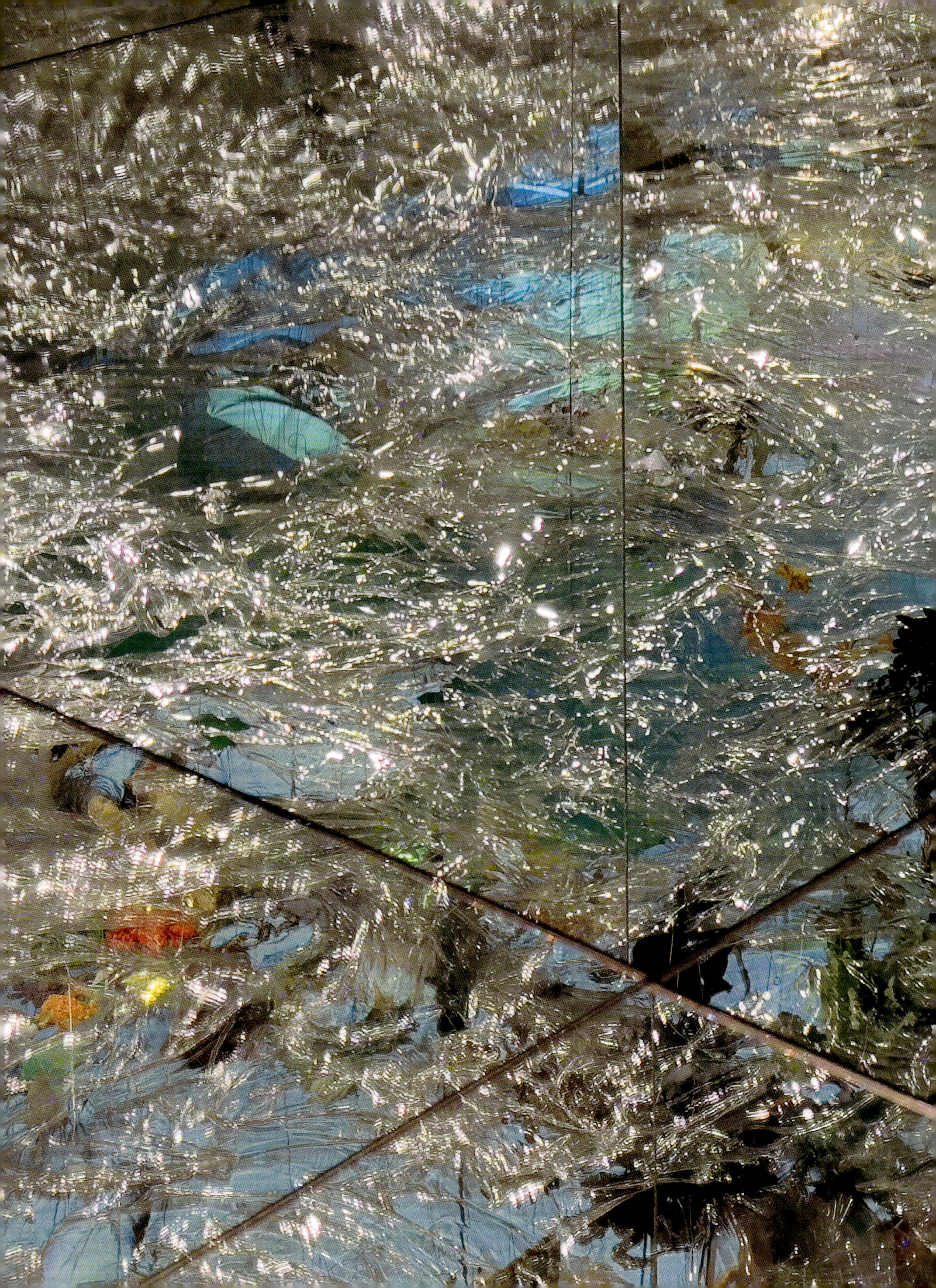

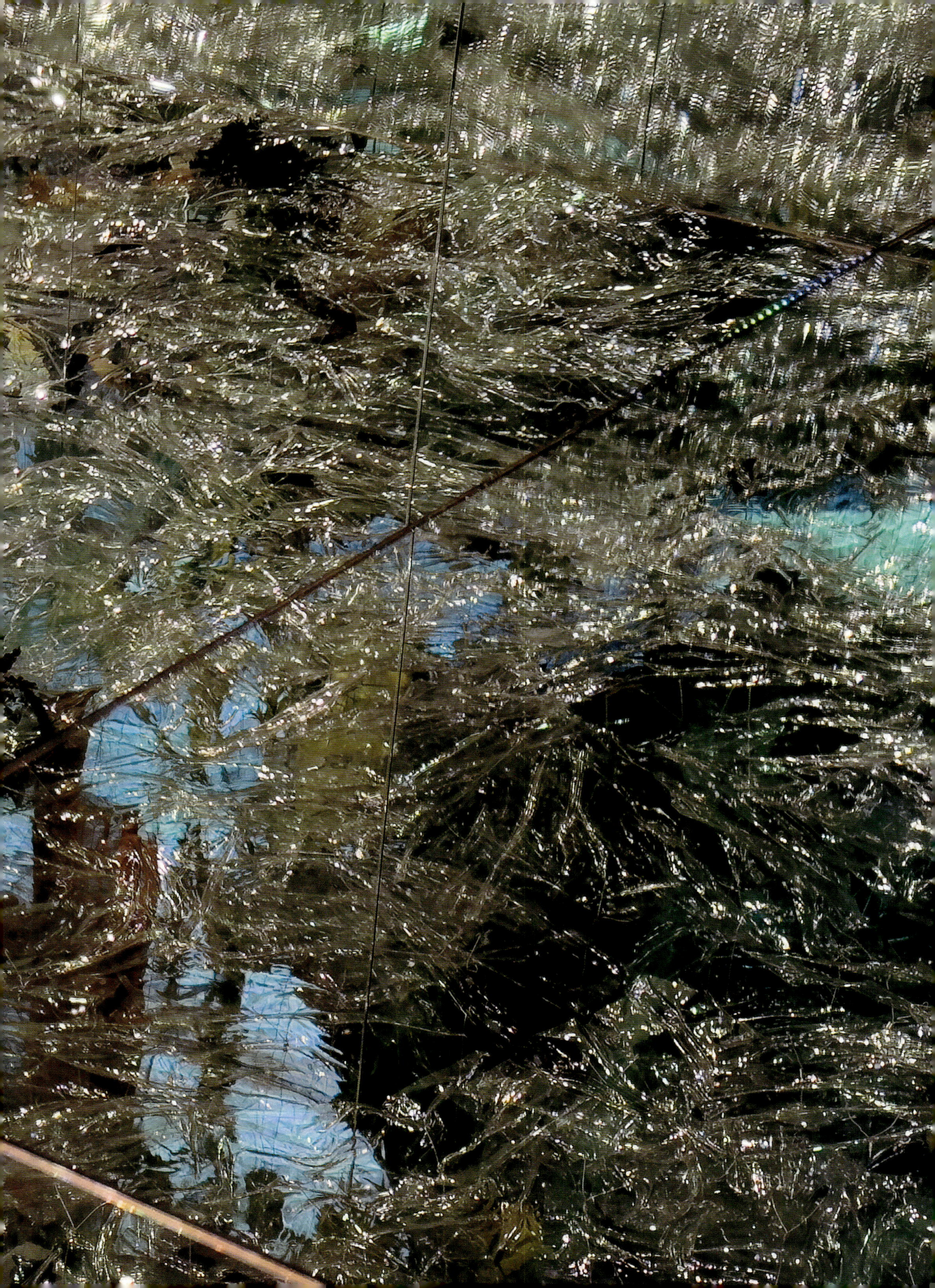

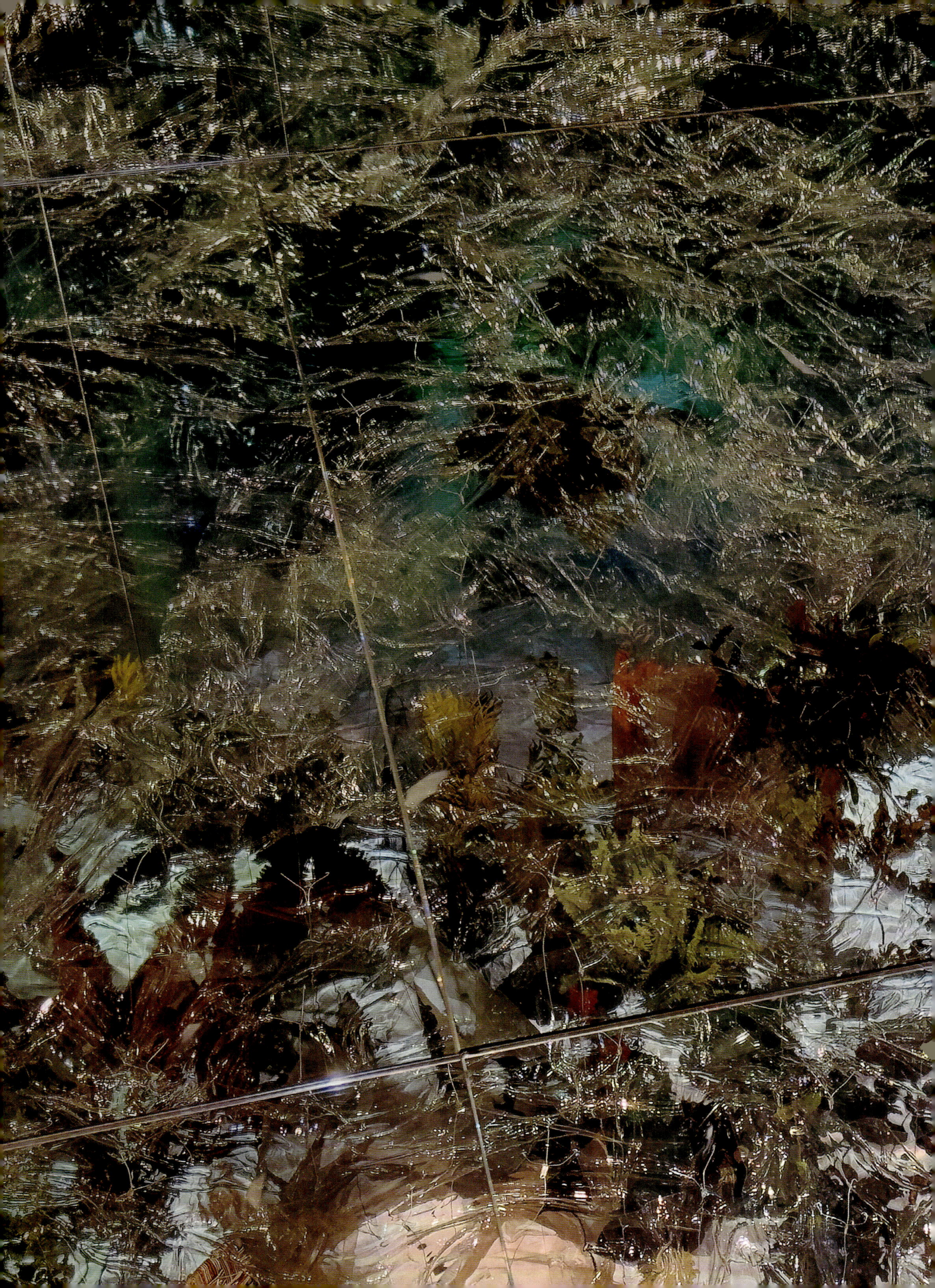

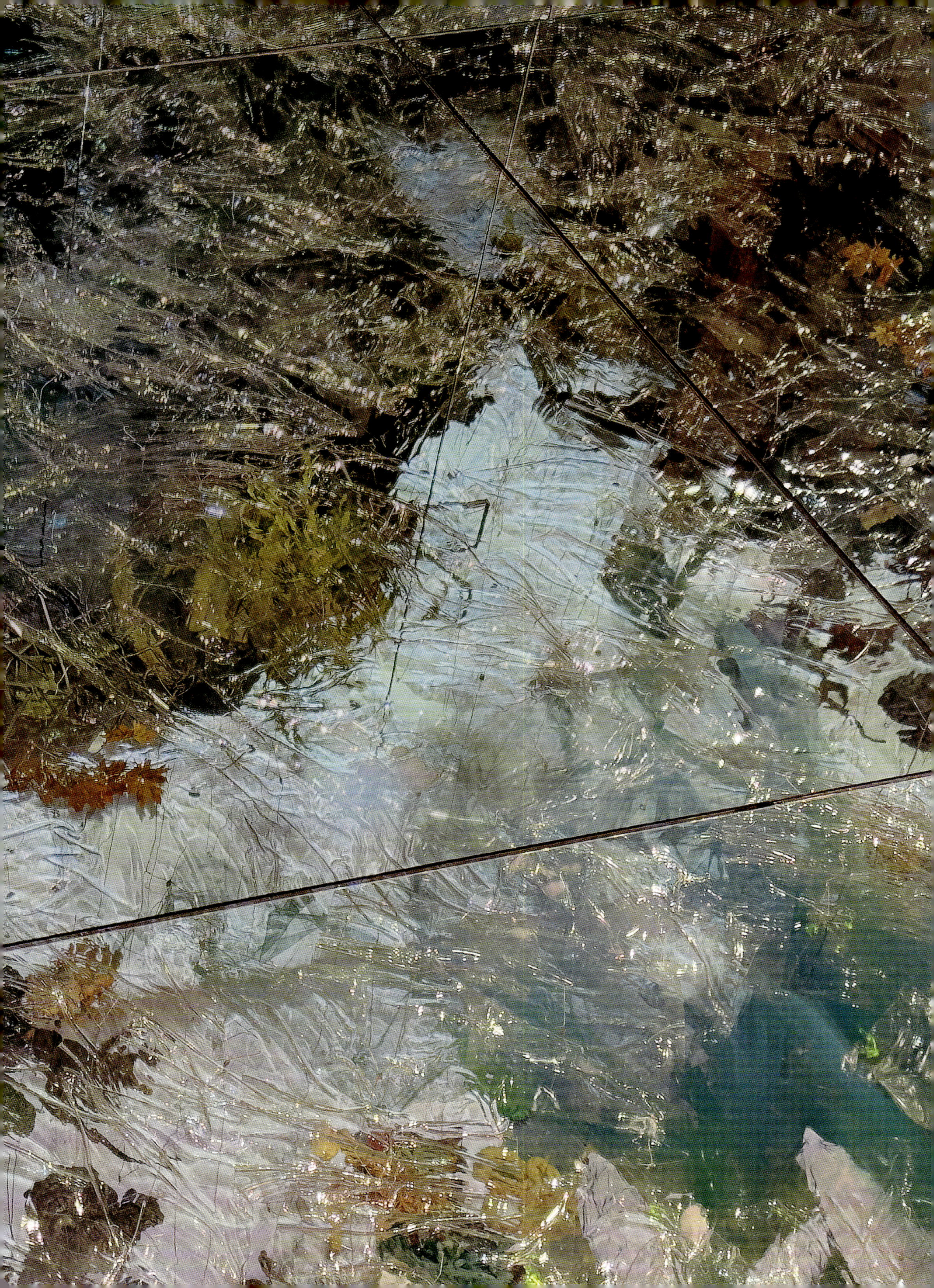

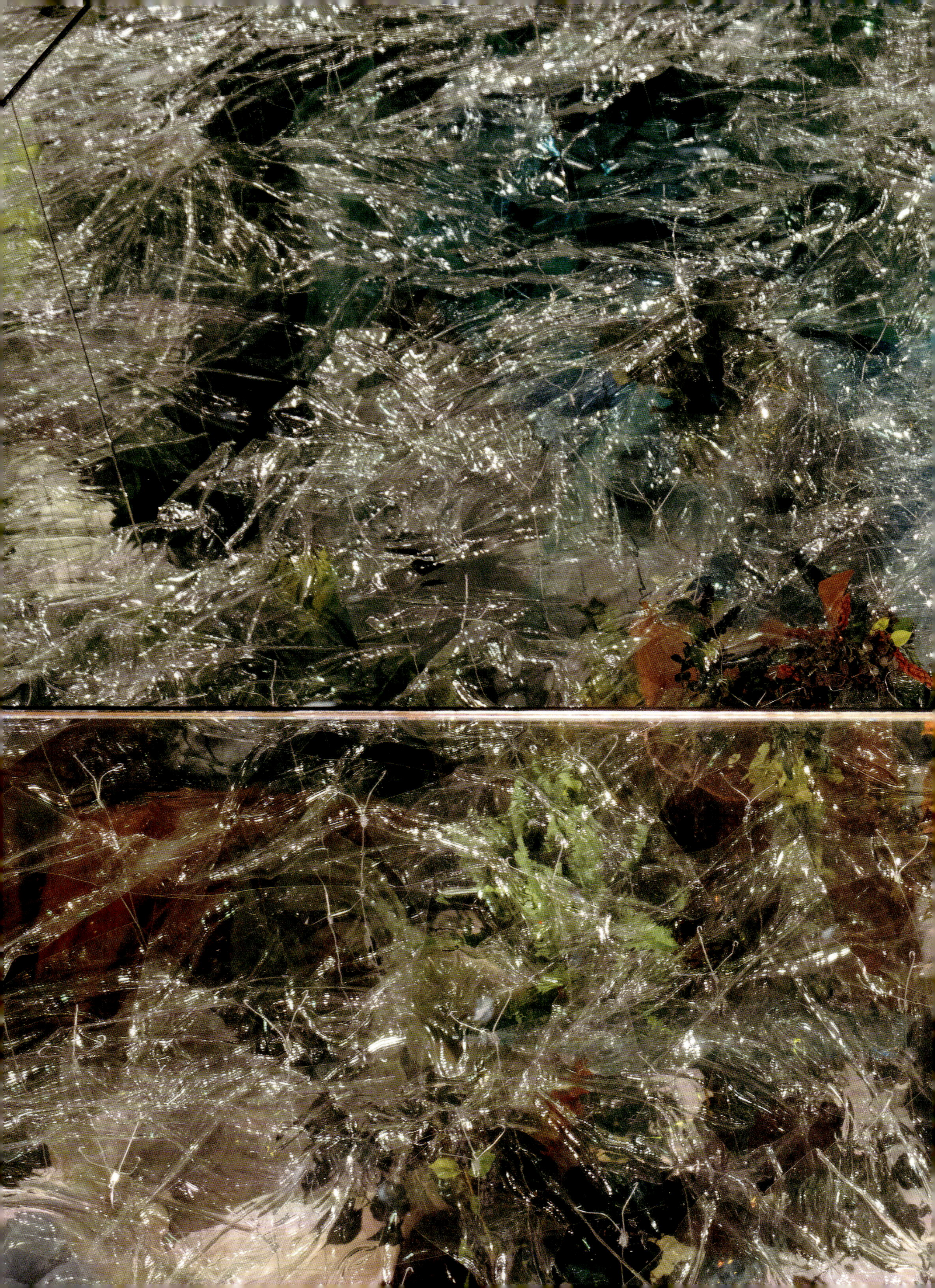

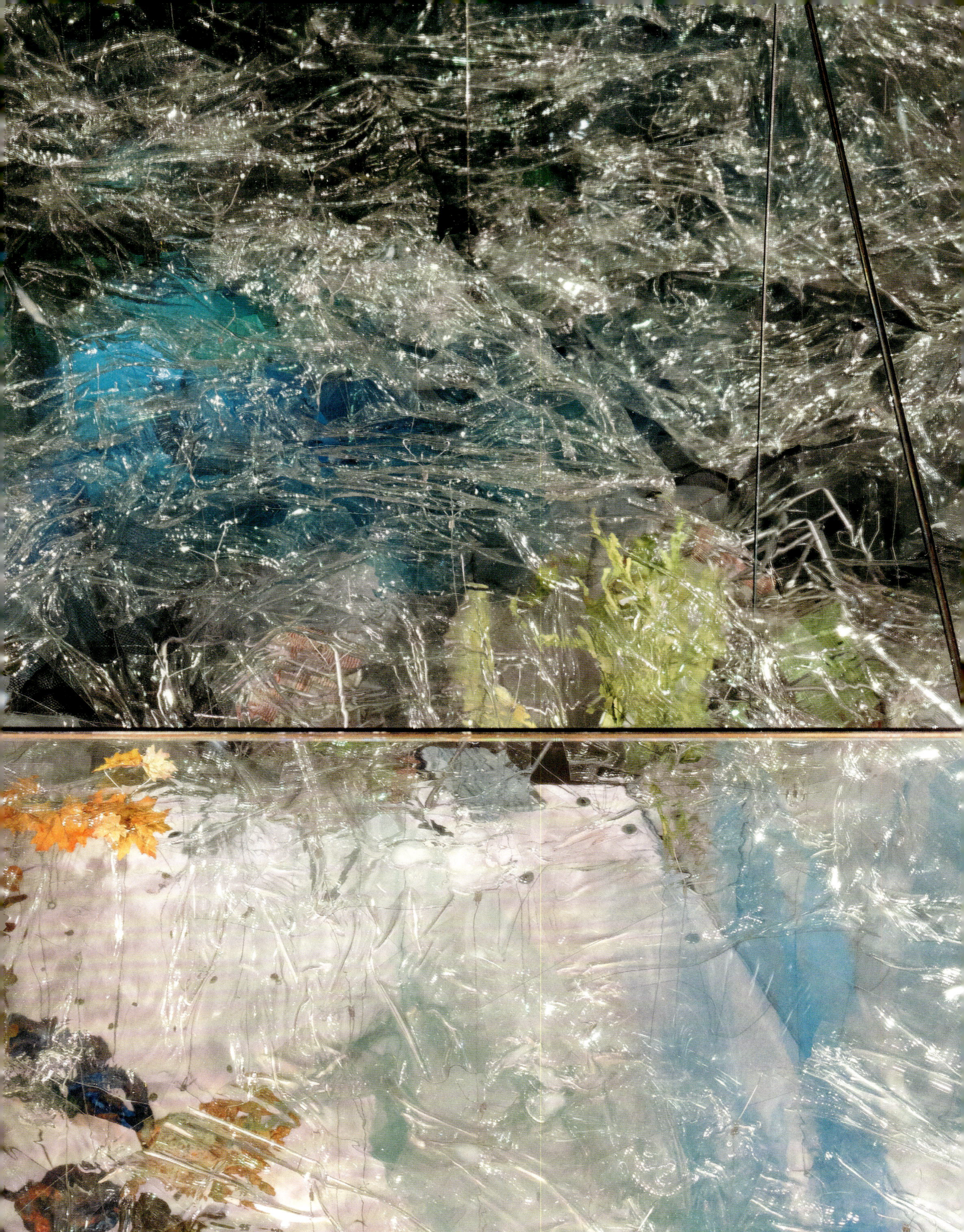

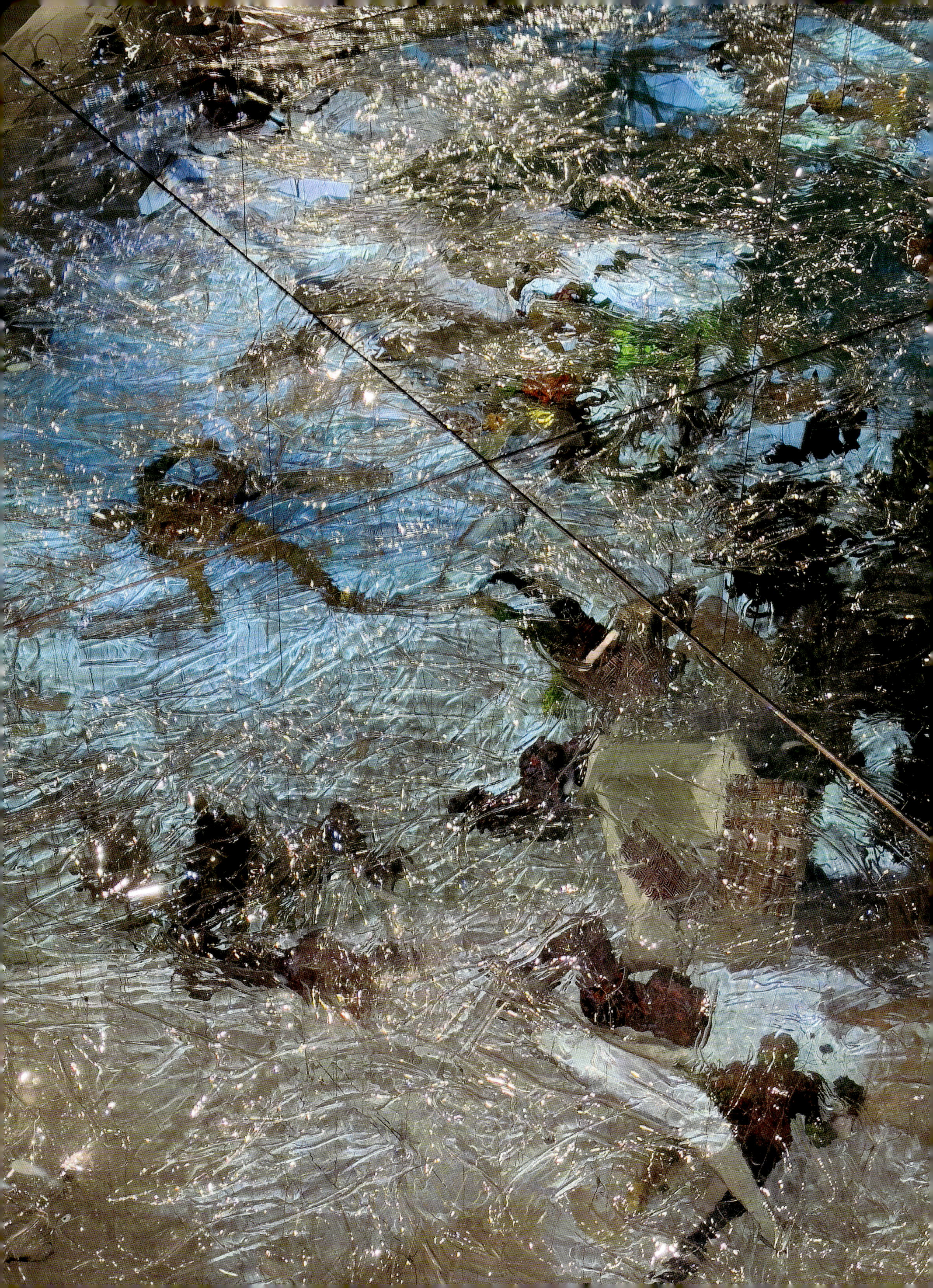

Without intention nothing would be made, yet there come inevitable points when reality overtakes it. Sometimes this comes as serendipity: raindrops. Often, the discrepancy is more complex. While improvisation is a central element in Golden's creative process, practical limitations also make it necessary. She has never had the resources to create an entire work, at scale, ahead of time. In the case of the Nasher, the relatively low height of the wedge-shaped room resulted in the ceiling's elements, intended for reflection in the mirrors below, being much closer to spectators on the viewing platform than she had anticipated.[17] Seen by simply glancing upward, her means had never before been so exposed, and it disturbed her. "Don't look up," she told one reviewer.[18]

While evoking nature and natural laws, *if earth is the brain then where is the body* does not attempt to create the model of an actual place in nature. It draws instead upon our perceptual and cultural mental files—and the bleed between them—to conjure a place that seems real, down to the pollution that populates it. That nature is not the model for this work is perhaps most apparent in Golden's resistance to symmetry, which she routinely referred to during installation as something that needed to be "broken." This was usually said of the Rorschach-like doubling created when sculptures were placed too close to the vertical mirrors, yielding straightforward reflections that immediately alerted the viewer to the illusion being created. She found ways to disrupt these, adding vegetation that interfered with the clear contours of a figure, reorienting others, and creating distractions exploiting the play of mirrors without calling attention to the symmetry their reflections inevitably reveal.

Golden's resistance to the visibility of the ceiling may also be understood in terms of her art's fraught relationship with symmetry. In the Nasher piece, the roughly circular shape of the body of water yielded by the mirror reflections possessed a lateral symmetrical balance. The intrusion of the ceiling risked generating a vertical symmetry as well, seen principally in the work of photographers who divided their compositions of her piece neatly between the reflections and their source, resulting in images of a deadening balance.

Visiting the exhibition near its end, Golden remarked that she still felt too close to the work's creation to assess it without reference to her original vision for it, which had not included the visibility of the ceiling and its components. As the exhibition's curator, I felt responsible to Golden to try and see the work as she did, or as she had imagined it. Yet the more time I spent in the gallery the more I began to see elements she considered shortcomings as not only intrinsic to the work but inextricably bound up in the meanings that it conjured. The lowering presence of the suspended sculptures became for me a kind of surrogate sky. For what else might the surface of the water be than a reflection of the sky above? I was reminded of a text by Anne Carson that beautifully evokes the dialectic between water and sky in a meditation on her brother's swimming habits:

> *Thursday 12:00 p.m. Swimming.*
> At noon the water is a cool bowl where the swimmer drops and darts away from the broiling air. He aligns himself and moves forward with his face in the water staring down at the bottom of the lake. Old, beautiful shadows are wavering steadily across it. He angles his body and looks up at the sky. Old, beautiful clouds are wavering steadily across it. The swimmer thinks about symmetries, then rotates himself to swim on his back staring at the sky. Could we be exactly wrong about such things as— he rotates again—which way is up? High above him he can feel the clouds watching his back, waiting for him to fall toward them.[19]

Looking at the intrusion of the ceiling into Golden's Nasher piece, I kept thinking of Claude Monet returning over and over to the permeability of water and sky in his *Nymphéas* paintings (FIG. 12), where waterlilies can appear to be floating in both. In the words of Carson's swimmer, which way is up? Golden began as a painter, and to a certain extent she still thinks like one, composing her installations intuitively, much as a painter might work on an expanse of canvas. She also paints the sculptures placed in her environments. The colors are often bright, almost garish, applied with a daubing, fractious brushstroke that can belie her figures' postures, whether curled into the fetal position of self-protection or fully extended, stiff-limbed.

For *if earth is the brain then where is the body*, Golden's compositional gifts had to operate on a level not demanded in painting. Not only did she have to compensate for sculptures being suspended above but viewed from below and for seeing them all in reverse via their reflections, she also had to consider their multiplied echoes in the circular space produced by the mirrors. Furthermore, the reflective and dichroic fabrics and their counterparts in fluorescent and interference paints changed the appearance of the sculptures

FIG. 12. Claude Monet, *Nymphéas*, 1903.
Oil on canvas; 28¾ × 36¼ in. (73 × 92 cm)

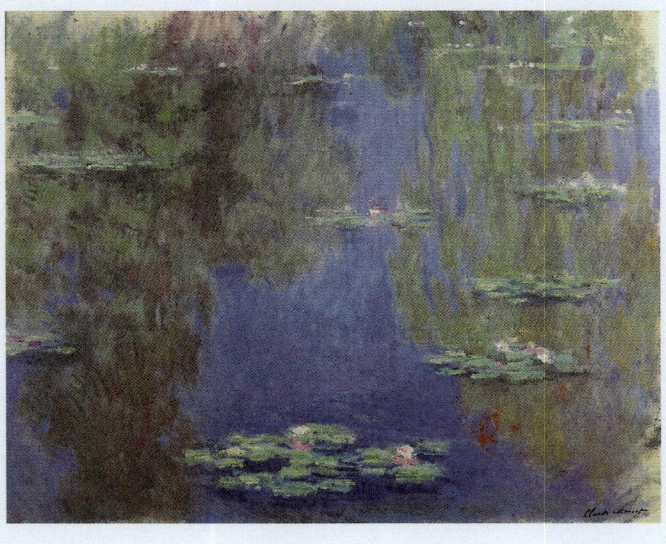

when seen in reflection, subject to different angles of light. This was complicated further by the shimmering plastic squares, which overlaid their own visual energy onto the composition as a whole.

The Impressionists gained their name from Monet's *Impression, Sunrise* (1872), a painting made by looking carefully at water and the effect of light upon it. The attempt to render the impression of such fugitive experiences would form one of the most persistent strains of modern art. Much of Golden's time during installation went to setting her water into motion so that it undulated, shimmered, and flickered—creating the very conditions that rendered water so tempting and yet so impossible to paint for Monet and others. Likewise, each of the little squares that Golden used for her wobbling, suspended waves became a kind of brushstroke.

Golden is often identified with the elaborate, viscerally expressive installations of such artists as Mike Kelley and Paul McCarthy, but something of these earlier painters and their continual, frustrated attempts to capture the sensation of a moment also lingers in her work. As sculptures, Golden's figures similarly share the nervous

FIG. 13. Medardo Rosso, *The Golden Age*
(*L'Eta d'oro*, also called *Aetas aurea*), late 1885–1886.
Wax over plaster; 19 × 18¼ × 14 in. (48.3 × 46.4 × 35.6 cm)

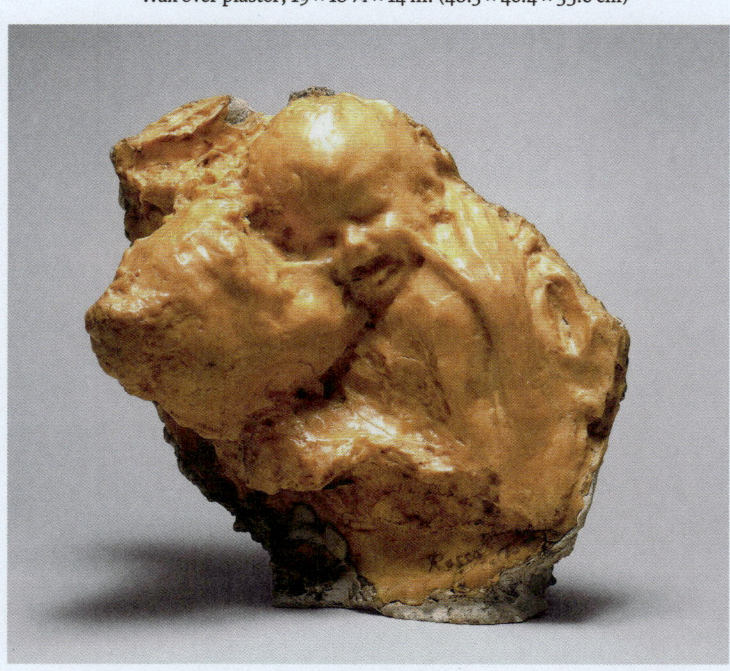

tactility of Alberto Giacometti's attenuated figures and the seeming fluidity of Medardo Rosso's gestural use of wax and plaster (FIG. 13), as well as these artists' wish to burrow inside an experience of perceptual immediacy. The difference for Golden is that these elements exist as part of a larger whole that seeks to provide a site for a multitude of such moments—working according to what she has described as "the idea of a place inside of a place."[20]

seeing is believing

Multiplied reflections of the handrail created the impression that it ran all the way around the body of water. From certain positions along the platform, however, this continuous line seemed to rupture and jump as it passed from one mirror to the next. This may have occurred due to minute discrepancies in the mirrors' installation—places where the floor may not have been perfectly level, for example—but it also touches upon an important parallel between mirror and water. In both cases, distortion is an inevitable part of perception. As light passes through water, it refracts, seeming to bend and break; likewise, as light strikes a mirrored surface, differences from the level of one piece of mirror to the next also lead to a perception of refraction. The distortion that appears in the line of the handrail disrupts that barrier's gently arcing line, but in a way that follows the rules of Golden's watery environment closely enough for our brains to adjust rapidly to the disruptions. Willem de Kooning, another artist who pondered how to capture the sensation of looking at water, teased apart optical experience and visual perception as he discussed the work of Piet Mondrian with the critic Harold Rosenberg:

De Kooning: I'm crazy about Mondrian. I'm always spellbound by him. Something happens in the painting that I cannot take my eyes off. It shakes itself there. It has terrific tension. The optical illusion in Mondrian is that where the lines cross they make a little light. Mondrian didn't like that, but he couldn't prevent it. The eye couldn't take it, and when the black lines cross, they flicker. What I'm trying to bring out is that from the point of view of eyes it's really not optical illusion. That's the way you see it. . . .

Rosenberg: The way you see something doesn't necessarily mean that that's the way it is. That business of putting a stick in the water so that it looks as if it's broken . . .

De Kooning: Well, it is. That's the way you see it.

Rosenberg: What do you mean, it is broken? If you pull it out of the water it's not broken.

De Kooning: I know. But it's broken while it's in the water.

Rosenberg: The break is an illusion.

De Kooning: That's what I am saying. All painting is an illusion.[21]

Refusing the reasonable argument that the stick remains whole all along, de Kooning returns, and holds onto, the flash of perception, the emperor's-new-clothes revelation of believing what he sees. Golden has likewise created a world in which these kinds of contradictory perceptions occur without disrupting the larger vision. This would likely not have been possible in her earlier works structured by means of architectural settings, which would have been utterly undone by such distortions. Instead, by taking water as her subject, Golden opened up a new way of thinking about mirrors and their metaphorical fluidity.

In the early development of Golden's Nasher piece, she envisioned an installation of water tumbling over different levels. She took inspiration in part from the cataracts of the Fort Worth Water Gardens (FIG. 14), which she visited during her first site visit to Dallas. Built by Philip Johnson and John Burgee in 1974, the park features an array of sharply angled, stepped levels over which waters cascade into a small, deep pool at its center. This site had been a key setting in the 1976 science fiction film *Logan's Run*, in which the two protagonists fled from their dystopian, enclosed city by passing through a range of aquatic environments—hot tubs, grimy pumping stations, and an icy cavern—before emerging on the Water Gardens' steps, surrounded by its tumult of waterfalls. Although she would leave this concept behind, its melding of an actual site with a cinematic version of it suggests the proximity of Golden's practice to film.

Golden has long recognized the connections between her art, film, and the city she now calls home:

> I have always been really inspired by film, when I was growing up in the '70s and '80s it seemed like every TV show, movie, and film was shot in [Los Angeles]. I wanted to see the fantasy, to see the cinematic possibility, and to be in a more expansive place.[22]

FIG. 14. Active Pool, Fort Worth Water Gardens, Fort Worth, Texas, ca. 2013

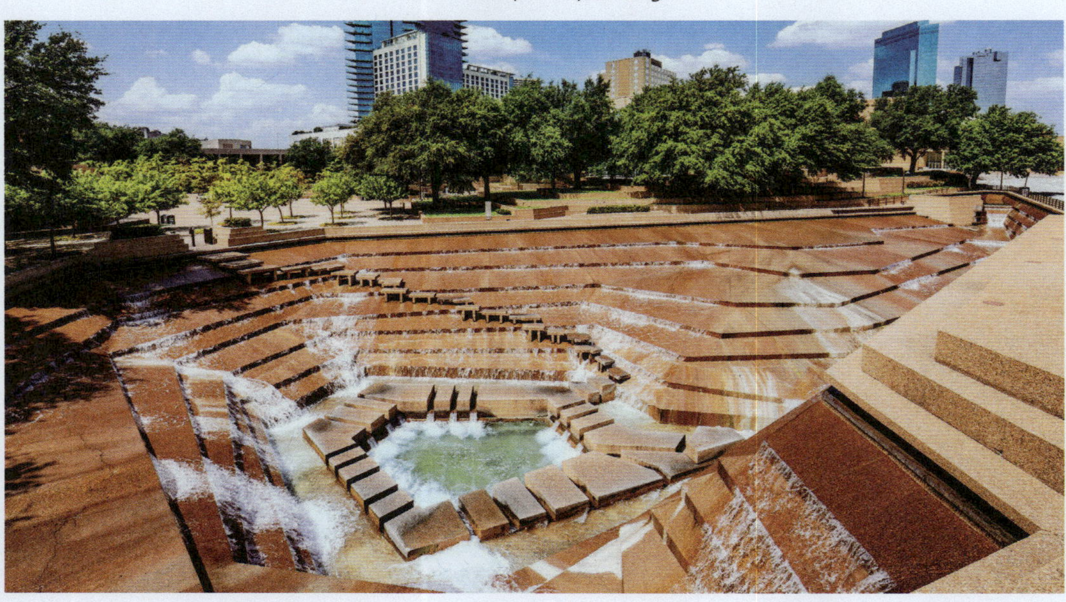

She has further identified film as a way of looking at her work as a whole:

> I like the idea that my whole life and all the installations I've made could be one long film, with each project as a scene or each perspectival view as a still. It makes me think of the way Jean Cocteau used film to explore time and space, which you can especially see in *Orpheus*. I love the idea that film can allow you to break into different dimensions and go from physical space to psychological space. . . . I really like the idea that the installations could be different places on one map, or different scenes in a film that I don't understand.[23]

As noted above, video has played a supporting role in a few of Golden's previous works, and in 2005 she also collaborated on *Sugar*, a full-length feature film.[24] The emotional and existential responses that her art can elicit have further prompted critics to make comparisons to films—including *Battleship Potemkin* (1925), *Being John Malkovich* (1999), and *Inception* (2010), among others—as a way to convey its effects.[25]

FIG. 15. Still (57:47) from Jean Cocteau, *Orpheus*, 1950

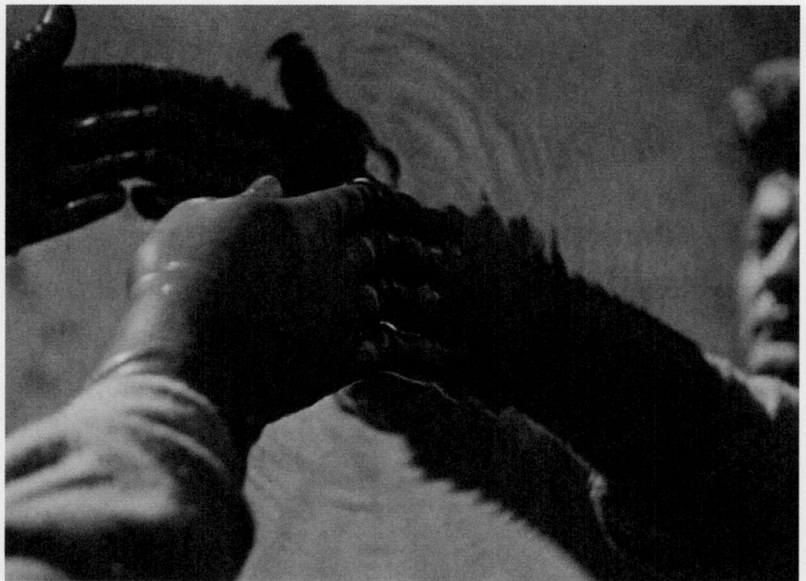

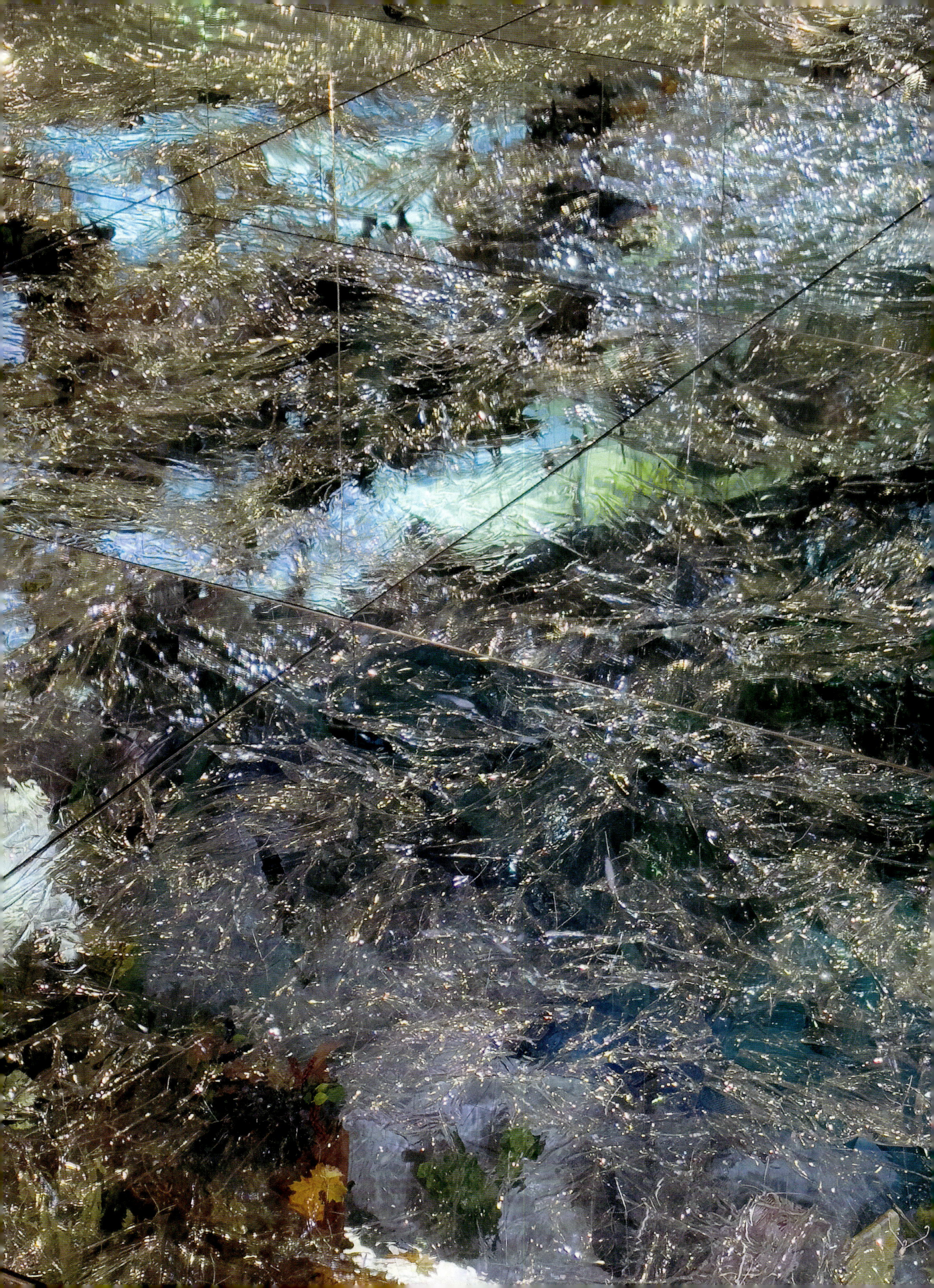

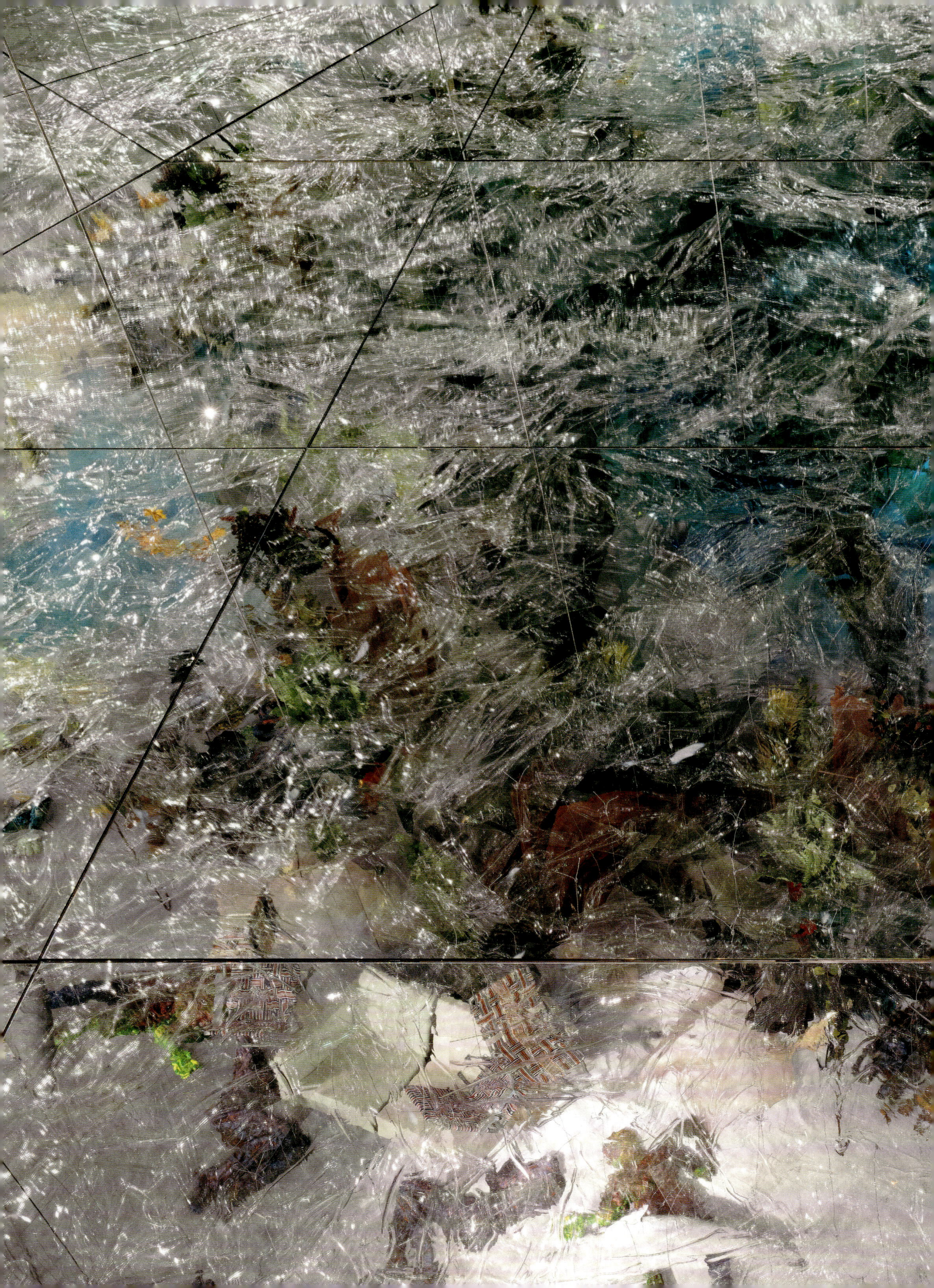

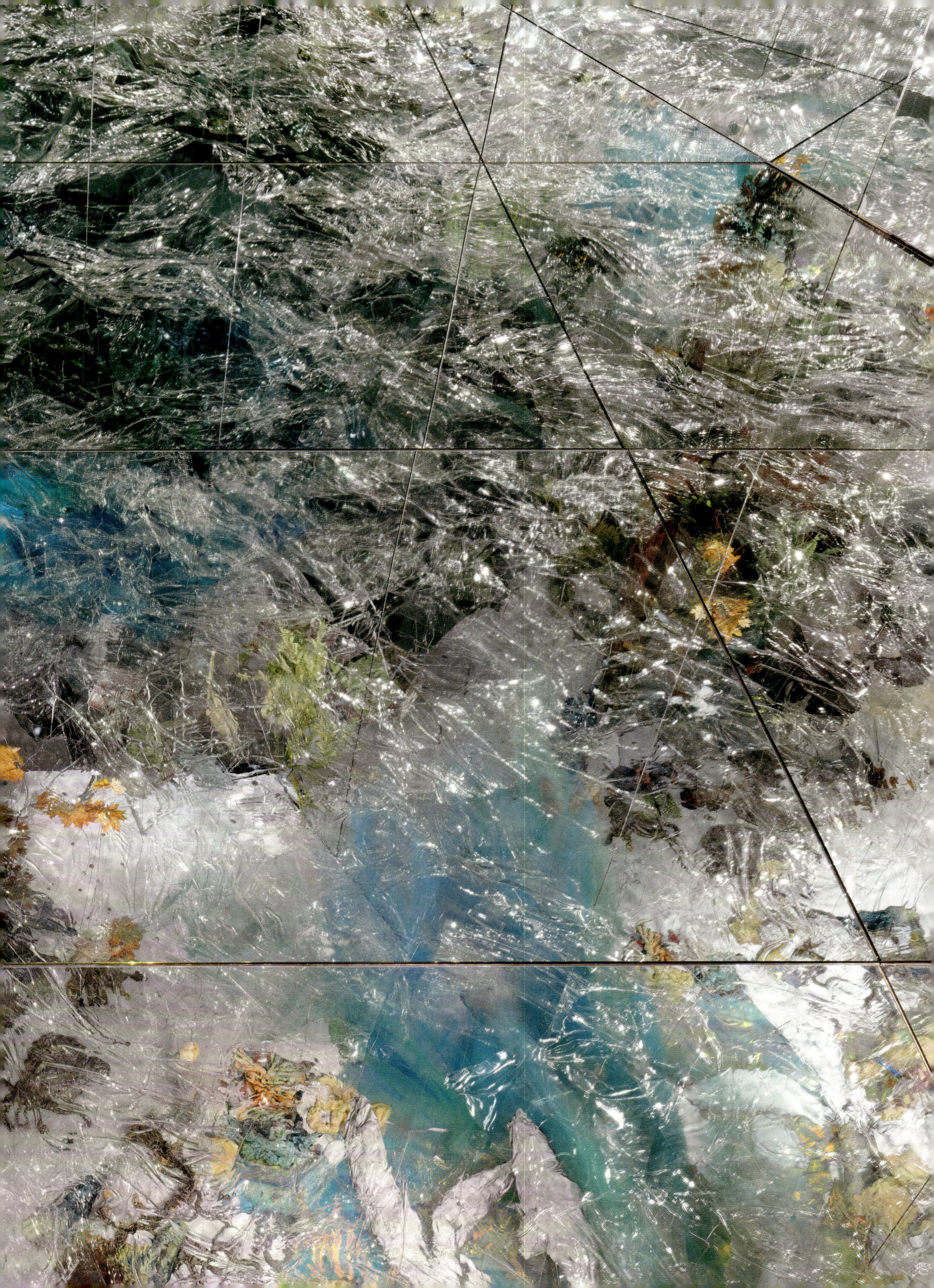

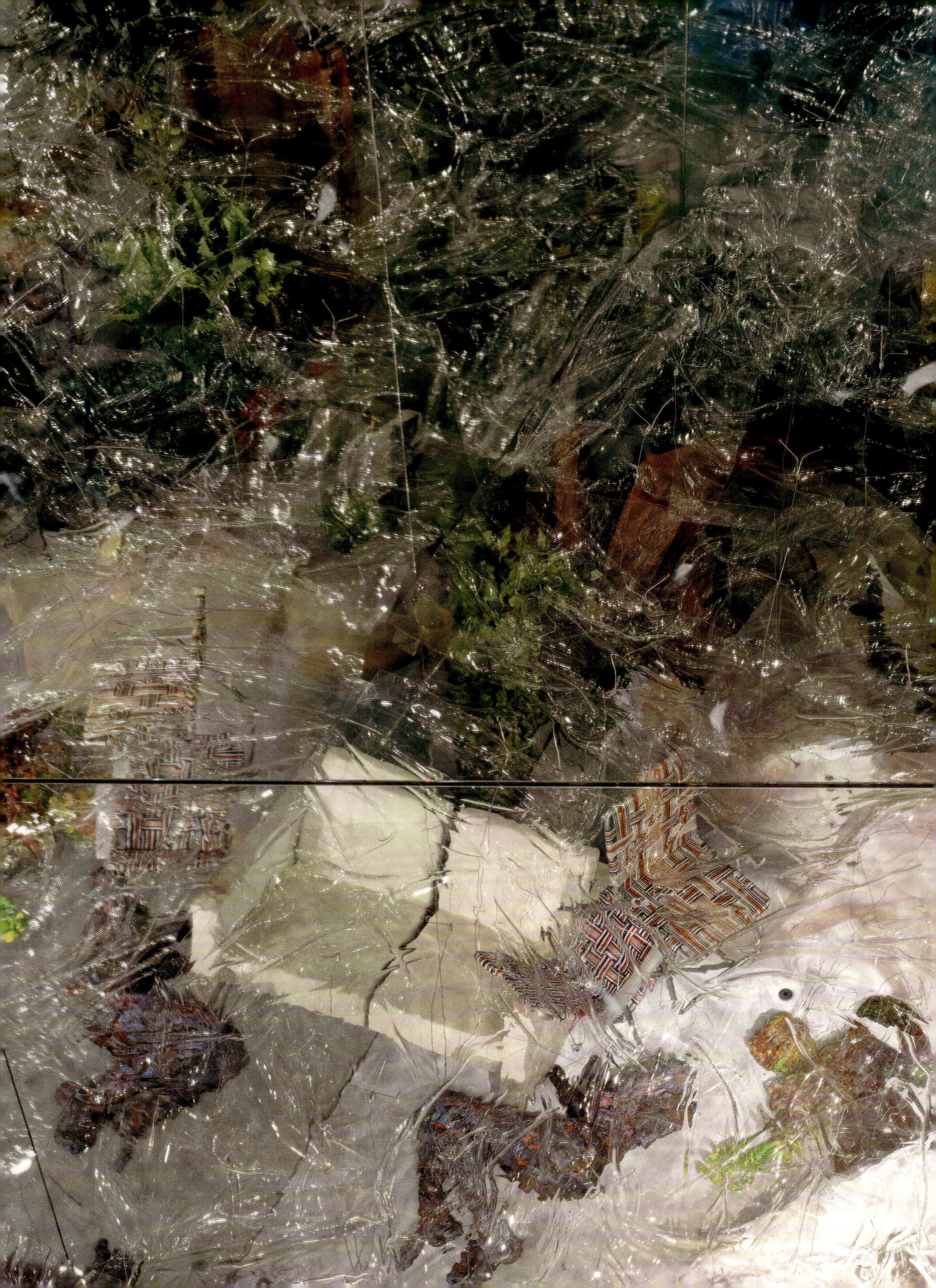

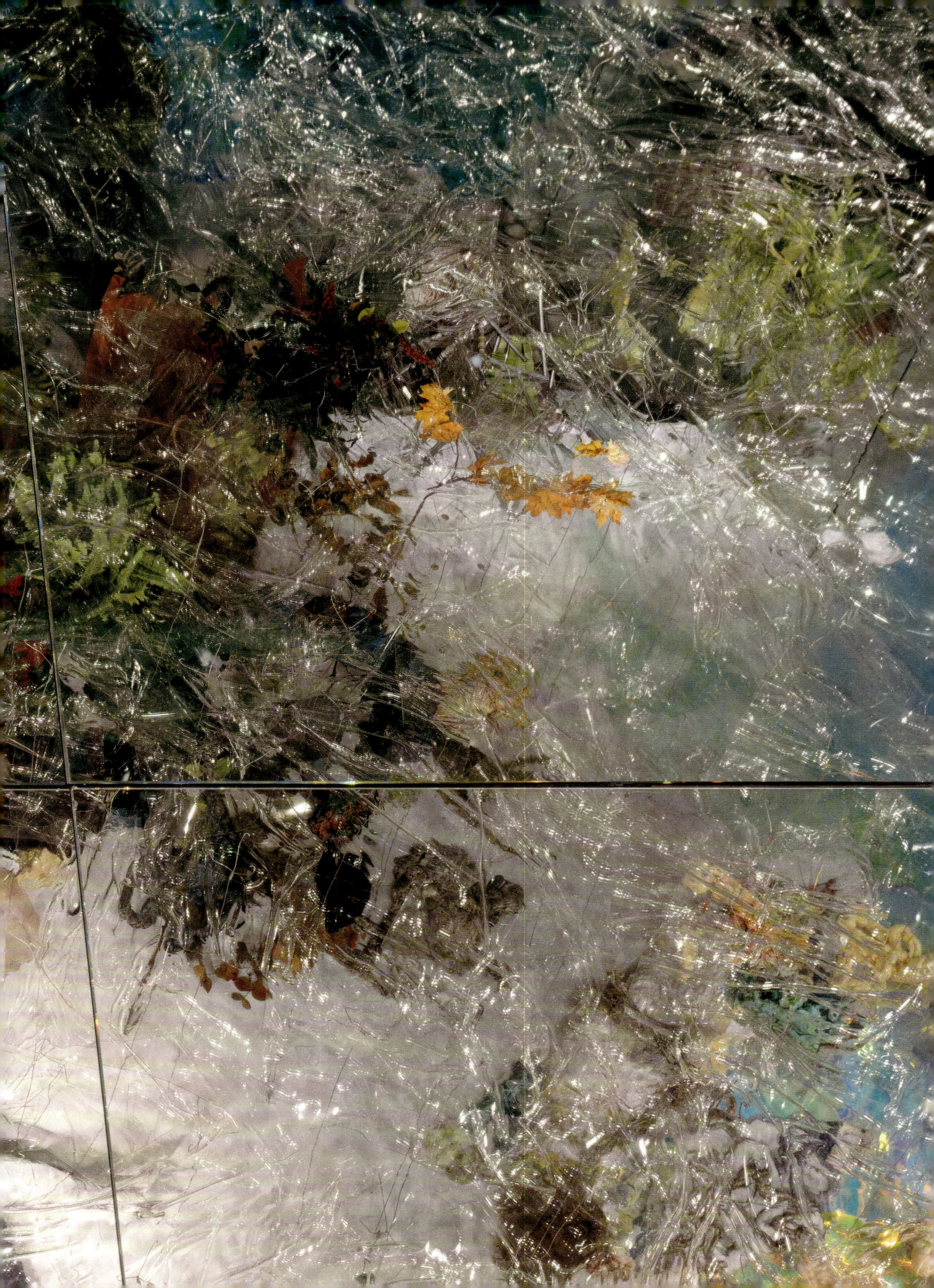

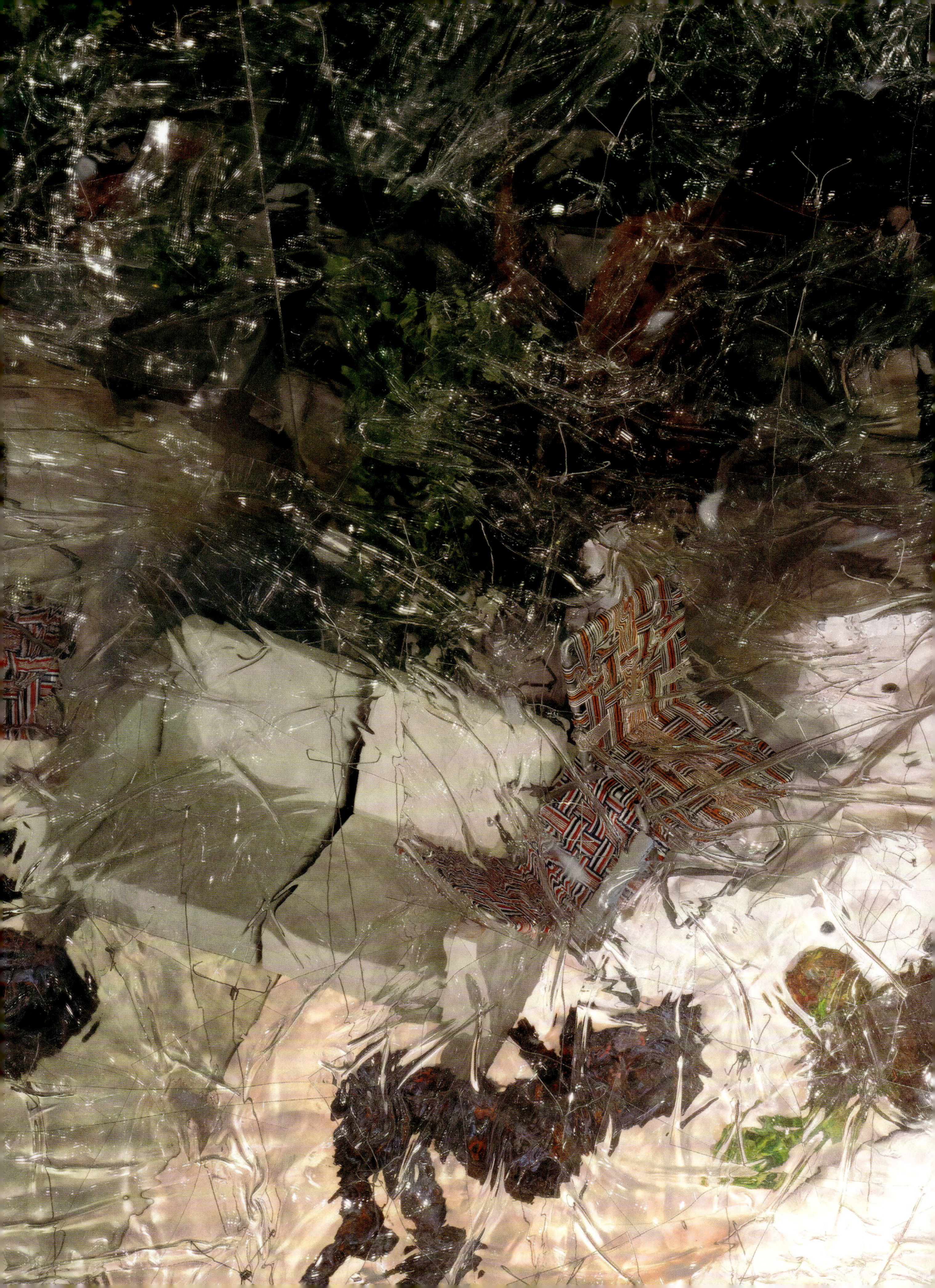

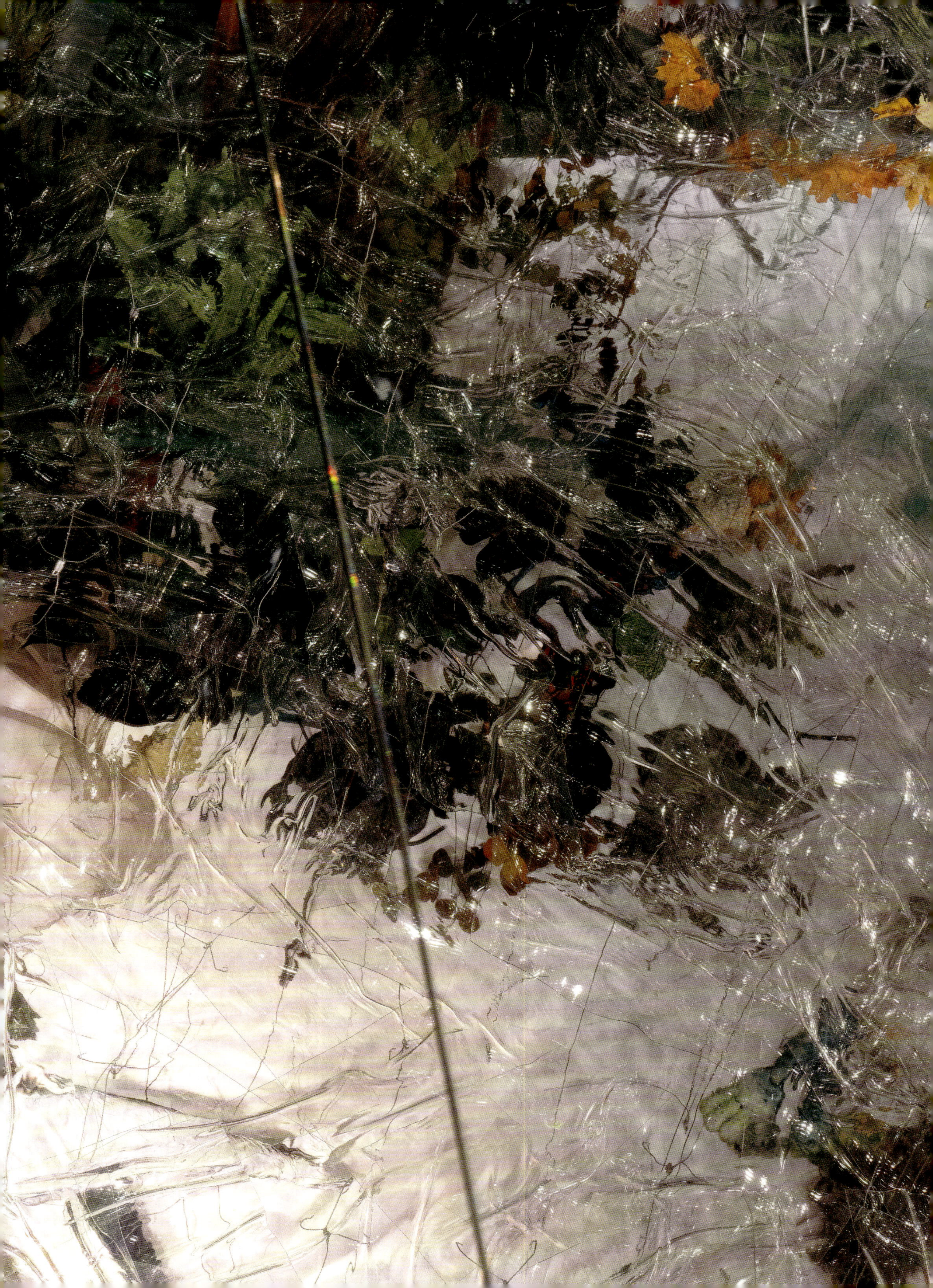

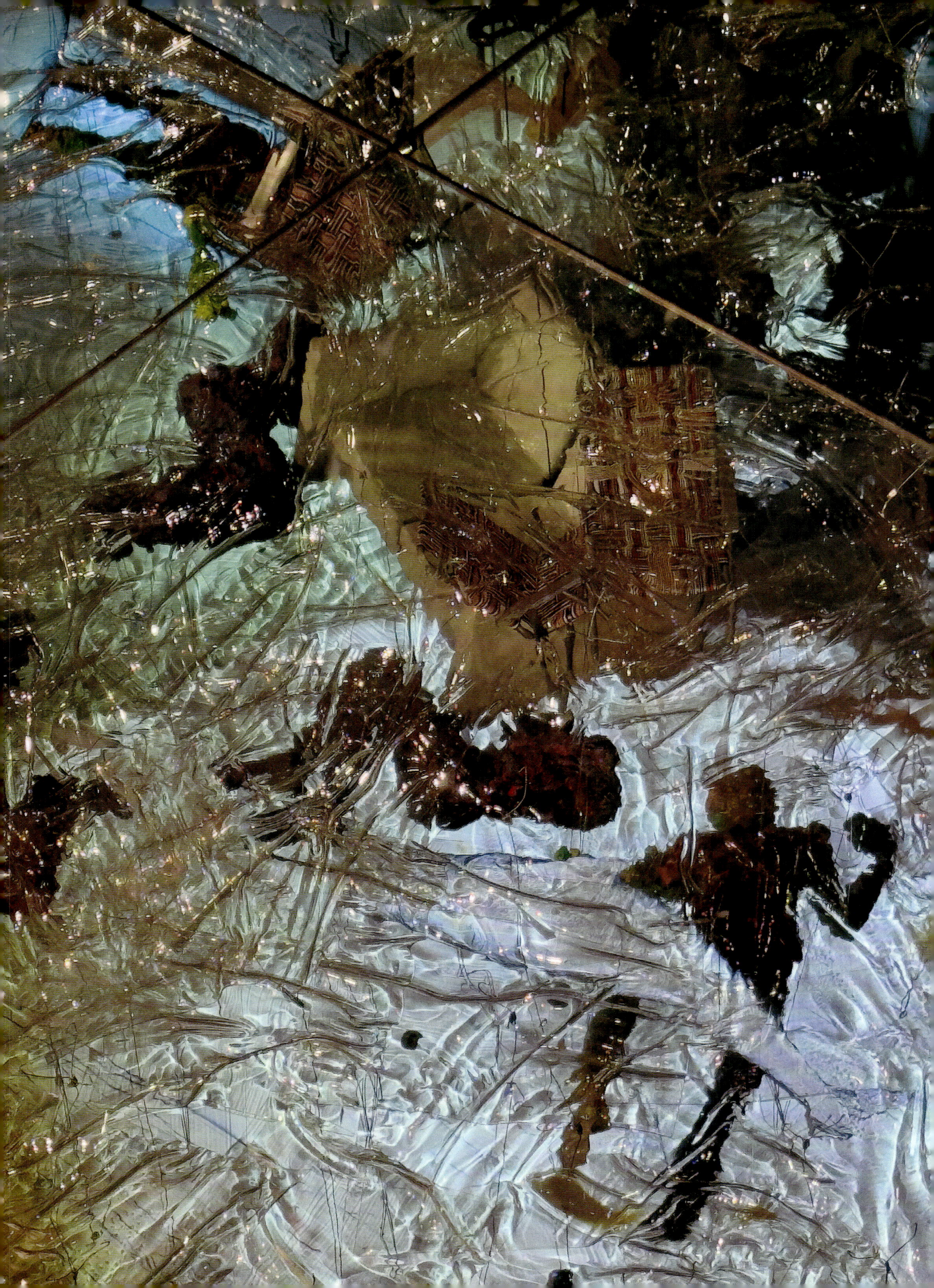

The relation of Golden's art to film becomes especially relevant in considerations of *if earth is the brain then where is the body*. Its melding of water and mirrors taps into a long tradition in film of mingling the two. In early cinema, mirrors were often used to film scenes that were difficult or dangerous for a live crew to capture, especially those like the underwater scenes of *20,000 Leagues Under the Sea* (1916). In *The Blood of a Poet* (1932) and *Orpheus* (1950), Jean Cocteau filmed voyages through a large looking glass by replacing the mirror at the last minute with a pool of water—a passage initiated with a sudden splash in the first film and a tentative delving of fingertips in the second (FIG. 15). Cocteau's use of a practical cinematic effect transformed the scenes into moments of magic.[26]

The multivalent associations of mirrors with bodies of water intensifies the impact of *if earth is the brain then where is the body*, heightening its ability less to fool the eye than to work on our emotions. Yet Golden is a visual artist, not a filmmaker, no matter how much inspiration films may provide. Much of her art's power resides in its compelling physical presence and the permission it gives the viewer to mentally traverse its environment, zooming in and out of details as no camera ever could. Even as her installation's existence moves into photographs, these in no way resemble film stills: they do not pluck an image out of a continuum so much as transfigure it into an object of memory, with all of the flattening, distortion, and reconfiguring that the act of remembering can hold.

lady in the lake

if earth is the brain then where is the body contained areas of remarkable beauty. On the right side of the piece, sea life and a single figure could be glimpsed through wavering lengths of seaweed. Brightly lit, animated with pale blues and greens, this area hinted at the paradisical sources of Golden's concept for a place of "release or relief," like the "fantasy of being on vacation."[27] Its counterpart is the swill dominating the installation's left side. A deeper ambivalence seeps through Golden's vision; like many people, she is afraid of water's power to engulf and pull us down, but she has also identified a more specific concern that haunts *if earth is the brain then where is the body*: "All through history and through films and books and everything, there's always a woman at the bottom of the river who's been killed."[28] Golden has recognized the "disgusting romanticism" of this trope—"a beautiful woman found underwater"—even as it fascinates.[29]

In addition to the fear of drowning, which can overtake anyone, women face additional dangers where water is concerned, including the possibility of sexual violence and death. Water's murky depths may aid in the hiding of a body, and its variable character, from unexpected visibility to the pull of currents, may reveal a body once submerged. Raymond Chandler gave a name to this genre in 1943 with *The Lady in the Lake*, a title subsequently used by Laura Lippman for her 2019 novel inspired in part by the murder of a Baltimore woman whose body was found in a fountain.[30] True crime podcasts, such as *Troubled Waters*, also attend to the dangers of water for women, and some of the most poetic, if grotesque, moments in film and television depend on such scenarios.[31] Dead but still achingly beautiful, Laura Palmer washes

FIG. 16. Still (45:29) from Charles Laughton,
The Night of the Hunter, 1955

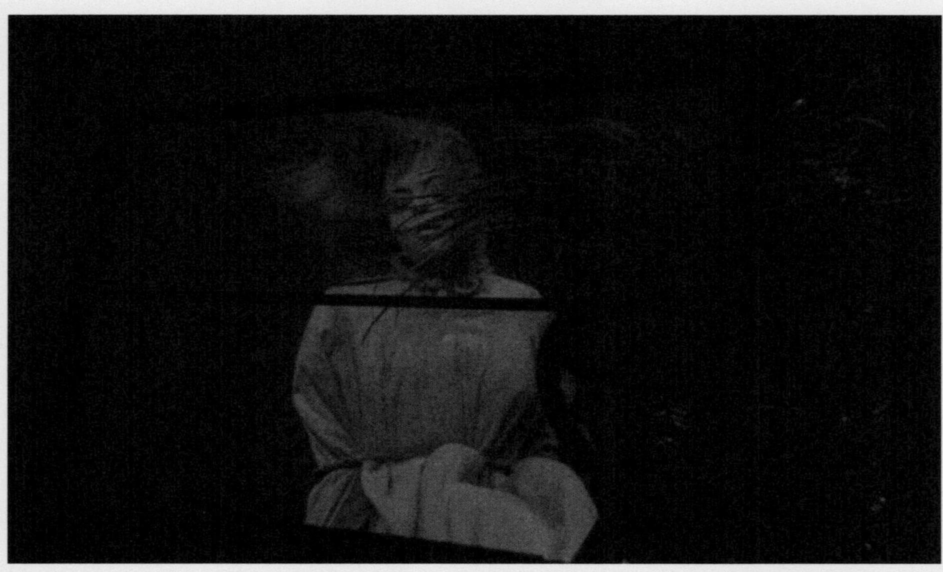

up on the shore of a lake, her naked body wrapped in plastic, in David Lynch's *Twin Peaks* (1990–91, 2007). In *The Night of the Hunter* (1955; FIG. 16), the fate of a female character is brought to light in the eerie image of her body tied to the passenger seat of an automobile sunk in the river; an underwater sequence reveals her first by showing long stretches of seaweed waving in the current, followed by the camera to the woman's corpse, her long hair likewise slowly undulating.

Seen from the distance of the viewing platform, none of Golden's figures could be identified with certainty as male or female. Yet their stasis amid other types of movement raised uneasy questions about them. Our culture has led us to expect that they might be dead, but Golden's installation offers no such narrative. Irresolvable, it provokes our awareness of the limits of our vision when confronted with the unknown: *if earth is the brain then where is the body* makes it difficult to see, both through the visual interference of the plastic waves and through the degree to which her piece's elements refuse to conform to the stories proffered by contemporary culture. The result became a kind of arena for fears, fantasies, and unanswerable questions.

fire

Golden made most of the sculptures for her exhibition in Los Angeles, then shipped them in bin boxes to Dallas. As the multifarious elements emerged, I was struck by two figures she referred to as "fire people," perhaps owing to the blazing red, yellow, and orange colors that seeped through darker layers of paint, like embers beneath ash. Her palette suggested strong emotion, given that we express our most intense passions in the language of fire: we can burn with desire as much as rage. Descending the Nasher's stairs and seeing the ringed, flickering lights within the darkened gallery created an initial impression of the infernal that never entirely dissipated. Along with the "fire people," chromatic flashes of magenta, chartreuse, and other colors here and there across the surface raised the specter of a circle of hell. When Satan and the rebel angels were expelled from heaven, John Milton's *Paradise Lost* (1667) conjured not a cavern or abyss to evoke hell but molten, flaming waters:

> he with his horrid crew
> Lay vanquisht, rowling in the fiery Gulfe
> Confounded though immortal . . .
>
> So stretched out huge in length the Arch-fiend lay
> Chain'd on the burning lake[32]

The hellish infiltrates but does not dominate *if earth is the brain then where is the body*. Golden's fire people lay on their sides, knees drawn up, in a partial fetal position, their vulnerability intensified by their initial placement, one nested against the other as if spooning. Their pose and the sculptural simplicity with which Golden rendered them recalled casts of Pompeian bodies trapped by volcanic ash. As installation progressed, and the fire people were separated and reoriented, their pathos turned to solitude. In turn, the infernal elements of Golden's piece remained only a disquieting undercurrent: her world is fallen but perhaps not damned.

murk

Golden's exhibition reminded one visitor of night fishing off a public dock, while another reminisced about snorkeling through pristine waters. Like many aspects of contemporary life, our experiences around water often involve class. What bodies of water can we access, and what can we do while we're there? In John Cheever's 1964 short story "The Swimmer," the main character has the quixotic idea to return to his suburban home from an equally affluent friend's house by swimming through all his neighbors' pools along the way. He takes off, joining backyard gatherings and accepting cocktails as he goes. A break in his carefully plotted itinerary requires him to traverse the public pool, a decidedly different experience:

> He took a shower, washed his feet in a cloudy and bitter solution, and made his way to the edge of the water. It stank of chlorine and looked to him like a sink. A pair of life-guards in a pair of towers blew police whistles at what seemed to be regular intervals and abused the swimmers through a public address system. Neddy remembered the sapphire water of the Bunkers' with longing and thought he might contaminate himself—damage his own prosperousness and charm—by swimming in this murk. . . . He dove, scowling with distaste, into the chlorine and had to swim with his head above water to avoid collisions, but even so he was bumped into, splashed, and jostled.[33]

During Golden's visit to the Fort Worth Water Gardens, she happened upon the "quiet pool," a lesser-known area of the park where the water appears still and unmoving. She was struck by the contrast between the famous cascading fountains and the opaque, seemingly stagnant water just on the other side of a high wall. Golden wanted her piece to encompass this type of experience as well—the fetid alongside the pure. Often these distinctions are structured in terms of class; the swill and broken furniture of her installation strongly suggest a down-market setting. A far cry from the golden sand and azure waters of popular fantasy, the discrepancies between reality and dream in Golden's piece might imply the presence of class differences in leisure, just as her earlier works contrasted the "good life" of a penthouse apartment with a hospital room or makeshift beds on heating grates. Yet *if earth is the brain then where is the body* brings this class anxiety into a place that all but overwhelms it: a body of water containing, in its murk, more than we can ever see or know.

Before deciding to structure her Nasher installation as a mirrored wedge, Golden tried models with mirrors going in different directions in the hopes of making what she envisioned as "an ocean or a water that would be endless to a horizon." When the logistics of planning such a space from the distance of her studio in Los Angeles proved too daunting, Golden simplified her vision yet worried that the result would "seem too much like a pool of water, like a Shamu situation."[34] Although the result clearly bore no resemblance to a swimming pool or a theme park like Sea World, a trace of its complex evolution lingered in Golden's assessment of the piece: "I like the way it ended up being a pool where it's about being stuck. . . . There has been a lot of stuckness in the process just figuring out how physically to make something non-physical happen."[35]

"Stuck," as Golden used it here, can be understood in the context of popular psychology, where it denotes experiences of being unable to progress or move forward. It has been claimed as an antonym to "flow," the prized mental state that characterizes unfettered, unself-conscious creativity.[36] Both terms draw upon figurative associations of movement, whether in people or in water. Within Golden's environment, stuckness appeared to prevail in the immobilized stillness of its inhabitants as much as its compositional containment. Yet there was movement as well, from the shimmering of currents to the flickering grace of occasional raindrops; even as the heart of the piece seemed to freeze up, its radiant blue-green light suggested a place of passage.

The "stuckness" of *if earth is the brain then where is the body* may be one of its most radical qualities. Whether through choice or necessity, being stuck can become a kind of resistance in a society that insists on constant striving and upward mobility, seizing on the cultivation of the flow state as a way to increase productivity. Those who experienced the Nasher piece had the opportunity to take their time, and many did, alone or in communion with others, often too caught up in what they were seeing to take out their phones. Golden's body of water, polluted and peaceful, domesticated and dangerous, offered a place to convene—to stop, ground, and look, and to be, for a time, stuck:

> My work is full of contradictions. I feel as if metaphorically this piece is about being stuck, so maybe it's good that I still haven't achieved an endless ocean because that's not the reality of my situation. I'm figuring out a puzzle for myself, and I want the viewer to do the same.[37]

Author's note: I am very grateful to a number of people whose help was invaluable during the course of this project. The Nasher's former Director Jeremy Strick had the vision to encourage me to pursue a project with Samara Golden, and our Interim Director and Chief Curator Jed Morse was indispensable in helping the artist and me navigate the logistics of building an entire world within a single gallery. Collaborating with Samara Golden to realize both her exhibition and this publication has been an inspiration and a pleasure. From beginning to end, my heartfelt thanks to Lewis Kachur.

1   Brian O'Doherty, *Inside the White Cube: The Ideology of the Gallery Space*, introduction by Thomas McEvilley (San Francisco: The Lapis Press, 1986), originally published as three articles in *Artforum* 14 (March, April, and November 1976). Regarding the architecture of the Nasher Sculpture Center, see Steven A. Nasher, ed., *The Nasher Sculpture Center Handbook* (Dallas: Nasher Sculpture Center, 2003).

2   *Sightings: Mai-Thu Perret*, March 12–July 17, 2016; *Sightings: Michael Dean*, October 22, 2016–February 5, 2017; and *Sarah Sze*, February 3–August 18, 2024. Perret's and Dean's exhibitions and one portion of Sze's were held in the Lower Level Gallery at the Nasher, Dallas.

3   Samara Golden, undated conversation with the author, circa January 2025.

4   For the 2023 Nasher Sculpture Center exhibition *Groundswell: The Women of Land Art*, Mary Miss created *Stream Trace: Dallas Branch Crossing*, a new work of Land art that brought attention to this submerged waterway and the various communities that had interacted with it before it was sent underground; see https://www.nashersculpturecenter.org/art/exhibitions/exhibition/id/1940/groundswell-women-of-land-art (accessed June 24, 2025).

5   Golden, text to the author, September 5, 2024.

6   Golden, in Sarah Lehrer-Graiwer, "An Interview with Samara Golden," in Mia Locks, *Samara Golden: The Flat Side of the Knife* (New York: MoMA PS1, 2015), 39.

7   Golden, email to the author, August 27, 2024.
     See also Golden's remark in *Samara Golden:
     Upstairs at Steve's* (Philadelphia: The Fabric
     Workshop and Museum, 2020), 31.

8   *Guts* was first shown at Night Gallery, Los Angeles,
     in 2022.

9   Golden, in Lehrer-Graiwer, "An Interview with
     Samara Golden," 40.

10   Golden, undated conversation with the author.

11   Golden talks about these aspects of her early life
     in Lehrer-Graiwer, "An Interview with Samara
     Golden," 39–40, 44.

12   Golden, in "Artist Talk: Samara Golden," a con-
     versation with Catherine Craft at the Nasher
     Sculpture Center, Dallas, September 28, 2024,
     https://www.nashersculpturecenter.org
     /read-watch/articles/article/id/354 (accessed
     June 24, 2025).

13   Golden, in Annabel Keenan, "Samara Golden,"
     Bomb, January 8, 2025, https://bombmagazine.
     org/articles/2025/01/08/samara-golden
     -by-annabel-keenan/ (accessed June 24, 2025).

14   Golden, in "Artist Talk: Samara Golden."

15   John Keats, "Ode on a Grecian Urn" (1819),
     collected in *John Keats: Complete Poems*, ed. John
     Stillinger (Cambridge, MA: Belknap Press,
     1982), 282.

16   Golden, in "Artist Talk: Samara Golden."

17   The height of the constructed space was twelve
     feet, but the viewing platform placed viewers
     about nine inches above the floor.

18   Samara Golden, quoted in Meka Boyle,
     "Don't Look Up," *Family Style*, November 7, 2024,
     https://www.family.style/art/samara-golden
     -nasher-sculpture-center (accessed June 24, 2025).

19   Anne Carson, "The Anthropology of Water;
     Water Margins: An Essay on Swimming by My
     Brother," in Carson, *Plainwater: Essays and
     Poetry* (New York: Alfred A. Knopf, 1995; first
     Vintage Contemporaries edition, 2000), 250.

20   Golden, quoted in Lehrer-Graiwer, "An
     Interview with Samara Golden," 41.

21   Harold Rosenberg, "Interview with Willem de
     Kooning," *Art News* 71 (September 1972): 56.

22   Golden, in Vera Neykov, "In the Golden Room,"
     Interview, October 7, 2013, https://www
     .interviewmagazine.com/art/samara-golden
     -the-fireplace (accessed June 24, 2025).

23   Golden, in Lehrer-Graiwer, "An Interview with
     Samara Golden," 40.

24   *Sugar* was directed by Patrick Jolley and Reynold
     Reynolds. See Andrew Berardini's descriptions
     and stills from the film in "Through the Looking
     Glass: Samara Golden," *Mousse* 35 (October–
     November 2012): 211–14.

25   For the *Battleship Potemkin* reference, see Cat
     Kron, "Samara Golden," *Artforum* (September
     2015): 372; *Being John Malkovich*: Jennifer S. Li,
     "Samara Golden," *Art in America* (April 15, 2014),
     https://www.artnews.com/art-in-america/
     aia-reviews/samara-golden-2-61694/ (accessed
     June 24, 2025); and *Inception*: Ken Johnson,
     "Samara Golden's New Point of View in 'A Fall of
     Corners,'" *The New York Times*, October 9, 2015,
     C23.

26   Cocteau also drew on the ancient myth of
     water-as-mirror from the tale of Narcissus, who
     becomes transfixed by his own watery reflection.

27   Golden, in "Artist Talk: Samara Golden."

28   Golden, in "Artist Talk: Samara Golden."

29   Golden, in Keenan, "Samara Golden."

30   Originally a figure of Arthurian legend, the Lady
     of the Lake provided King Arthur with his sword
     Excalibur. In *The Lady in the Lake* (1943),
     Raymond Chandler borrowed the reference for
     his novel, in which the body of a missing woman
     is discovered in a lake, and the term became
     associated with the murder of women. The novel
     was adapted in 1947 as a film. Laura Lippman's
     Lady in the Lake (2019) was adapted as a
     miniseries in 2024.

31   *Troubled Waters* was a ten-part podcast devoted
     to the 2011 death of a young woman whose body
     was found in a creek.

32   John Milton, *Paradise Lost* (1667; 2nd ed., 1674),
     book 1, lines 51–53 and 209–210; available
     as a Project Gutenberg eBook prepared by Joseph
     Raben (February 1, 1992), https://www.gutenberg
     .org/cache/epub/26/pg26-images.html
     (accessed June 24, 2025).

33   John Cheever, "The Swimmer," *The New Yorker*
     (July 18, 1964), 31, available at https://www
     .newyorker.com/magazine/1964/07/18/the
     -swimmer (accessed June 24, 2025).

34   Golden, in "Artist Talk: Samara Golden." Shamu
     was the name used for a series of orcas at Sea
     World theme park; the original Shamu died in
     1971 after six years in captivity.

35   Golden, in "Artist Talk: Samara Golden."

36   The psychologist Mihaly Csikszentmihalyi
     pioneered the theory of this concept in his book
     Flow: The Psychology of Optimal Experience
     (New York: Harper and Row, 1990), and it
     rapidly passed into popular psychology and
     memes.

37   Golden, in Keenan, "Samara Golden."

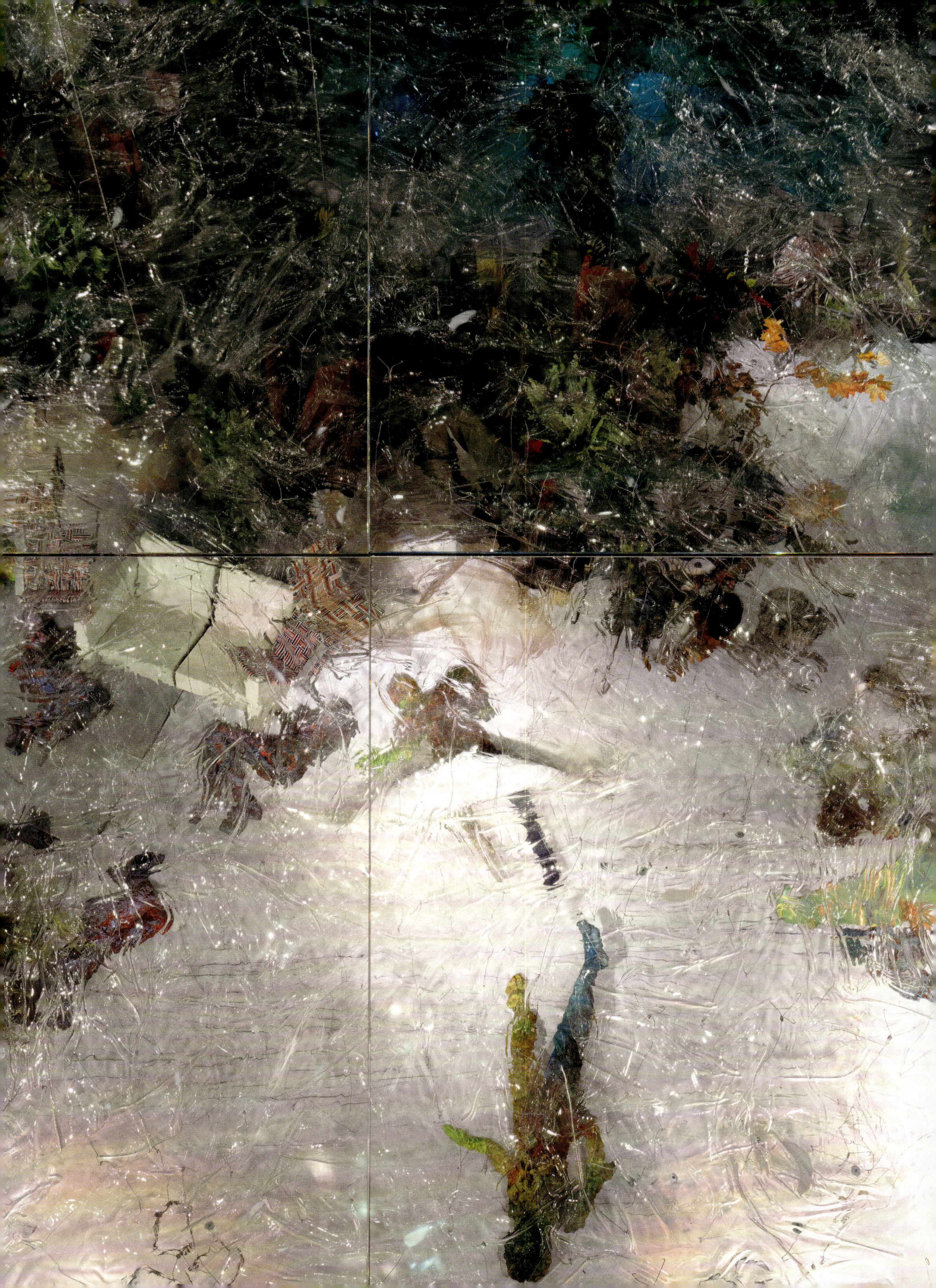

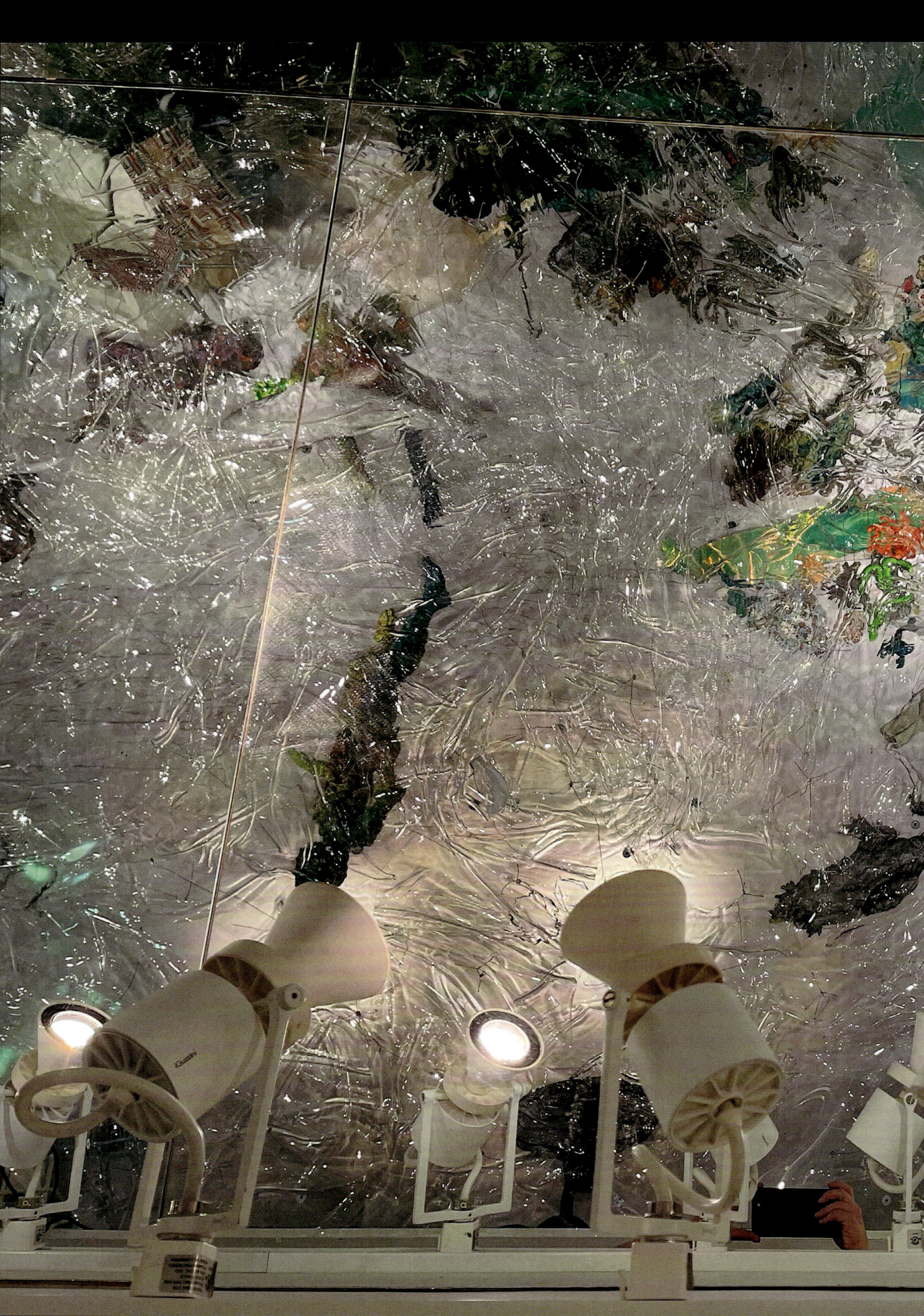

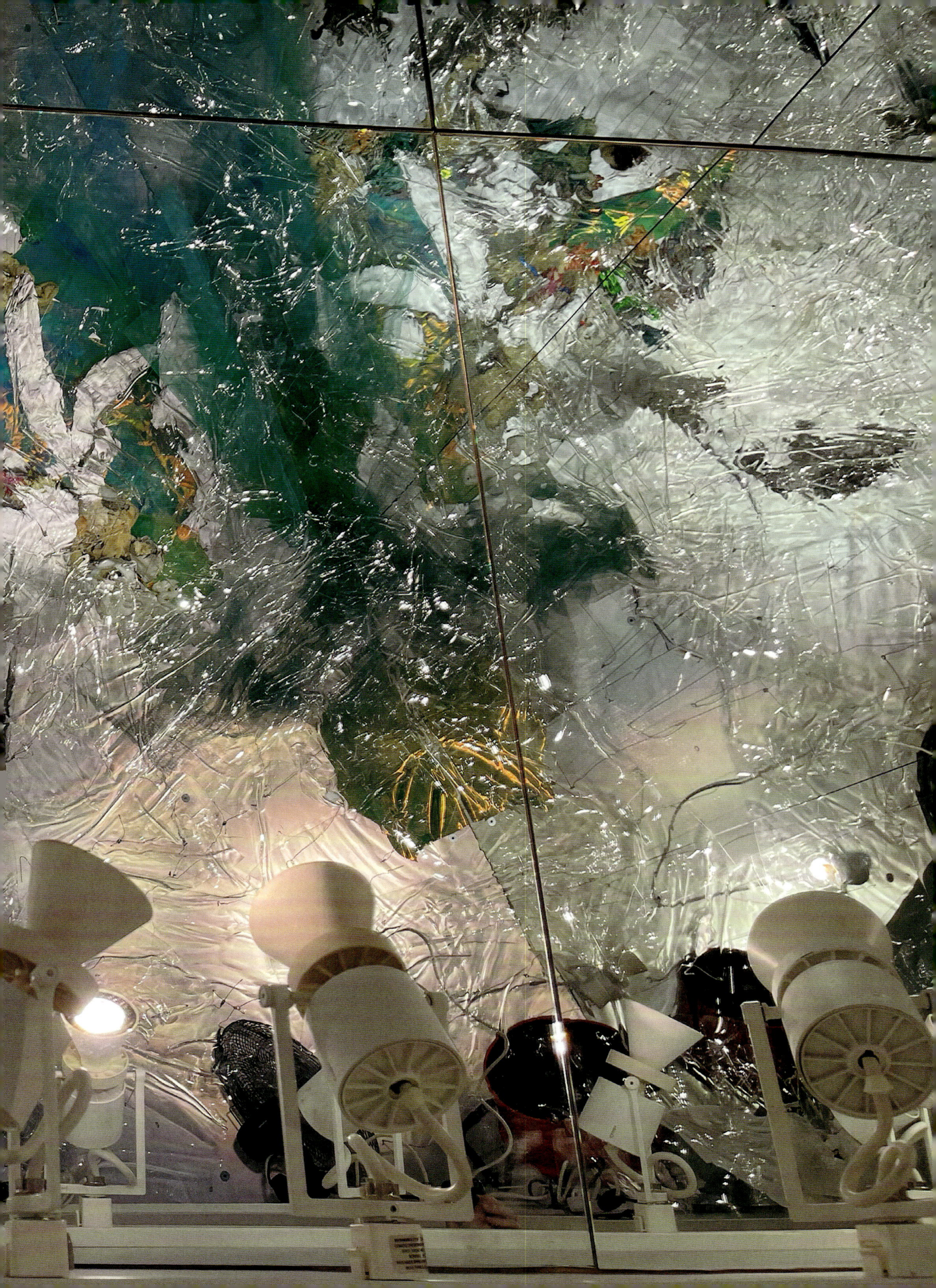

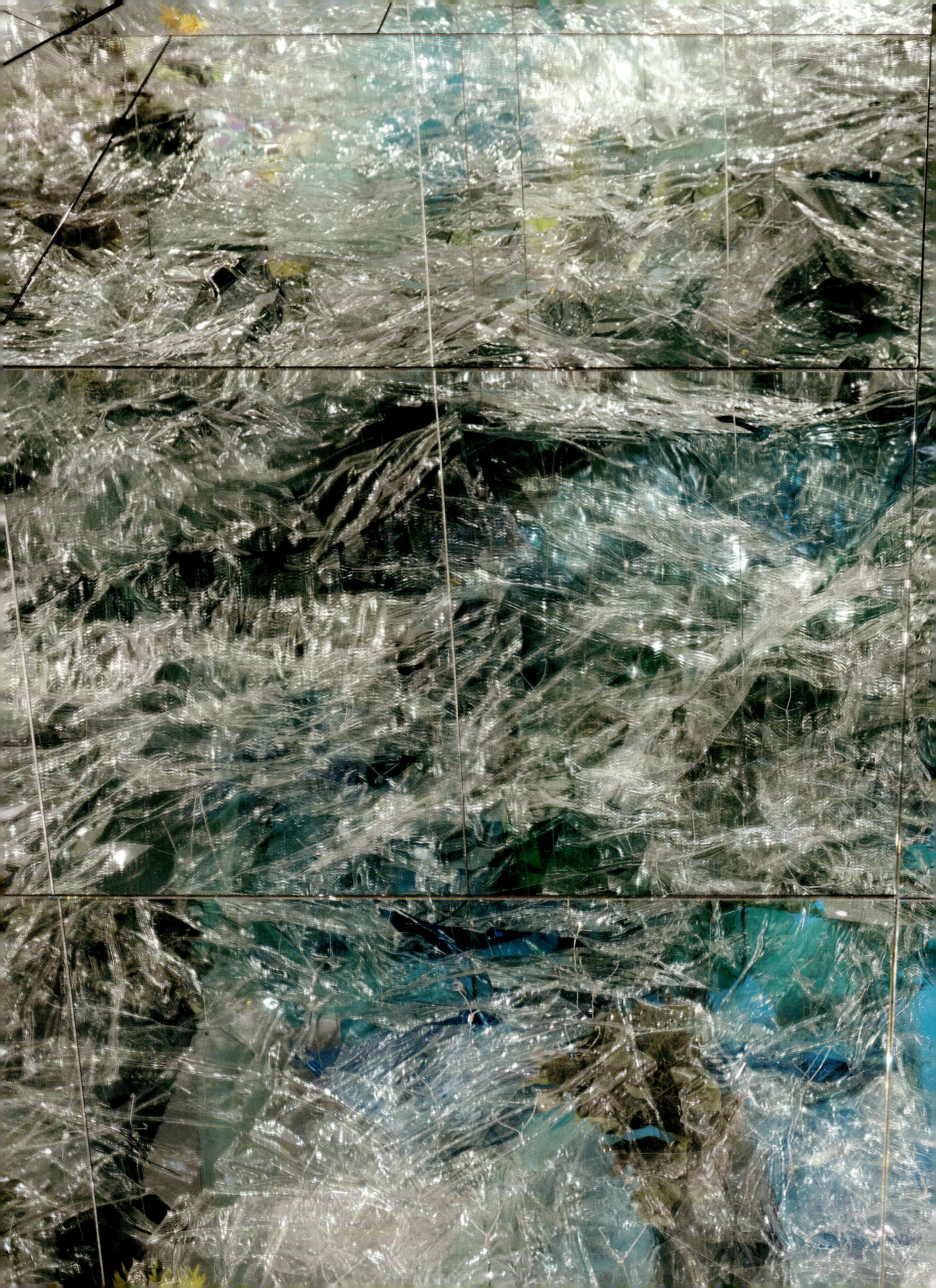

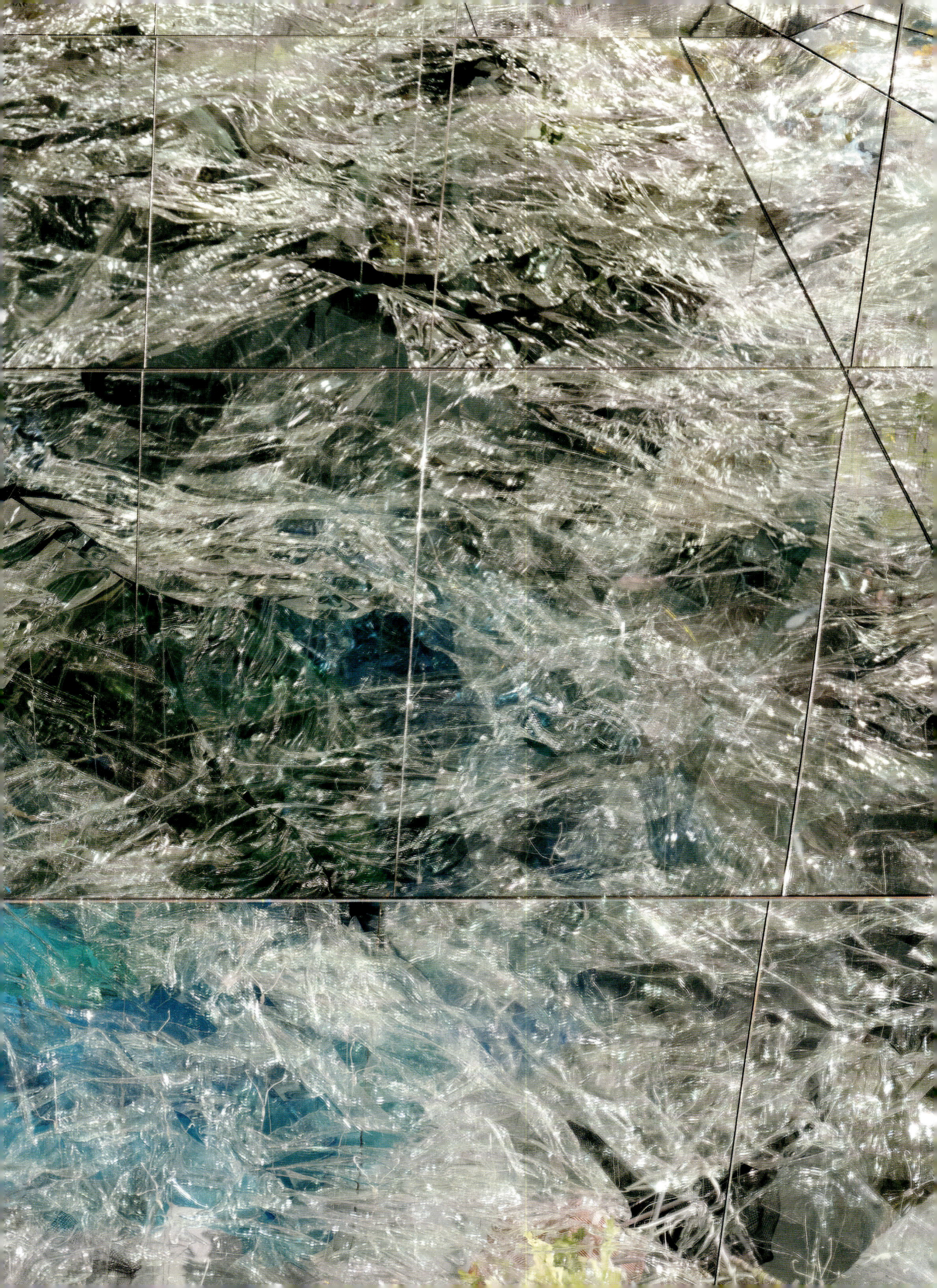

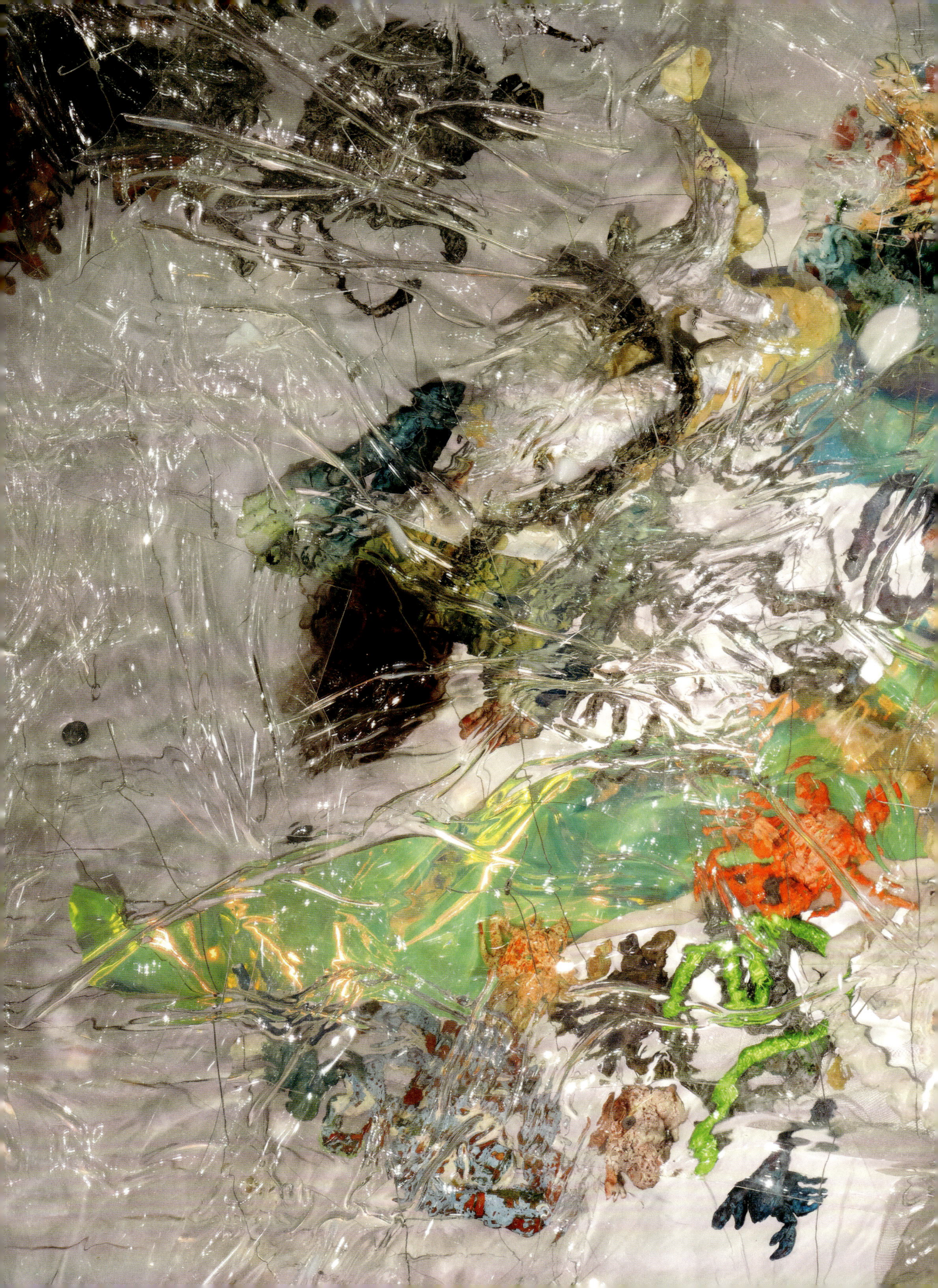

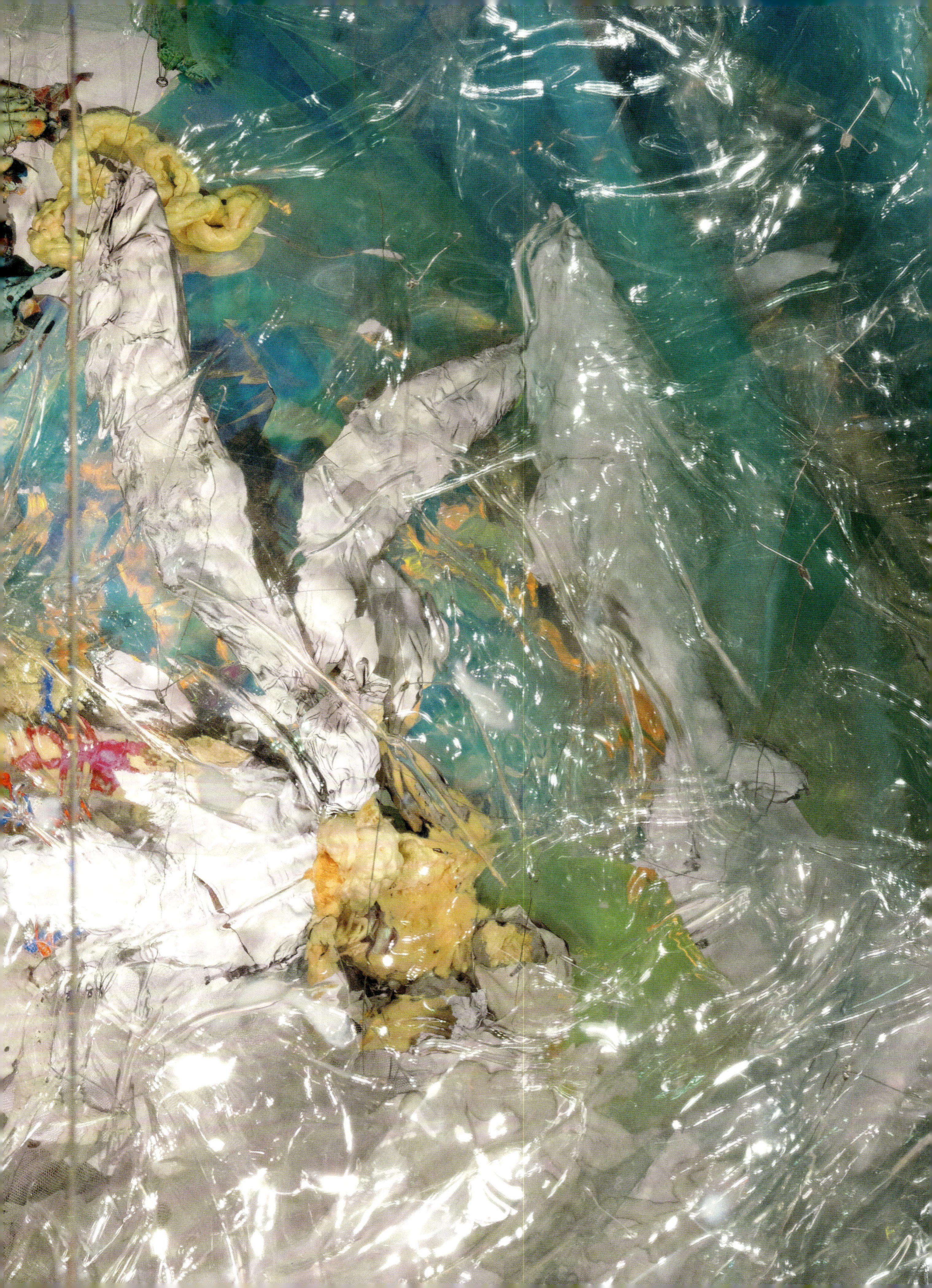

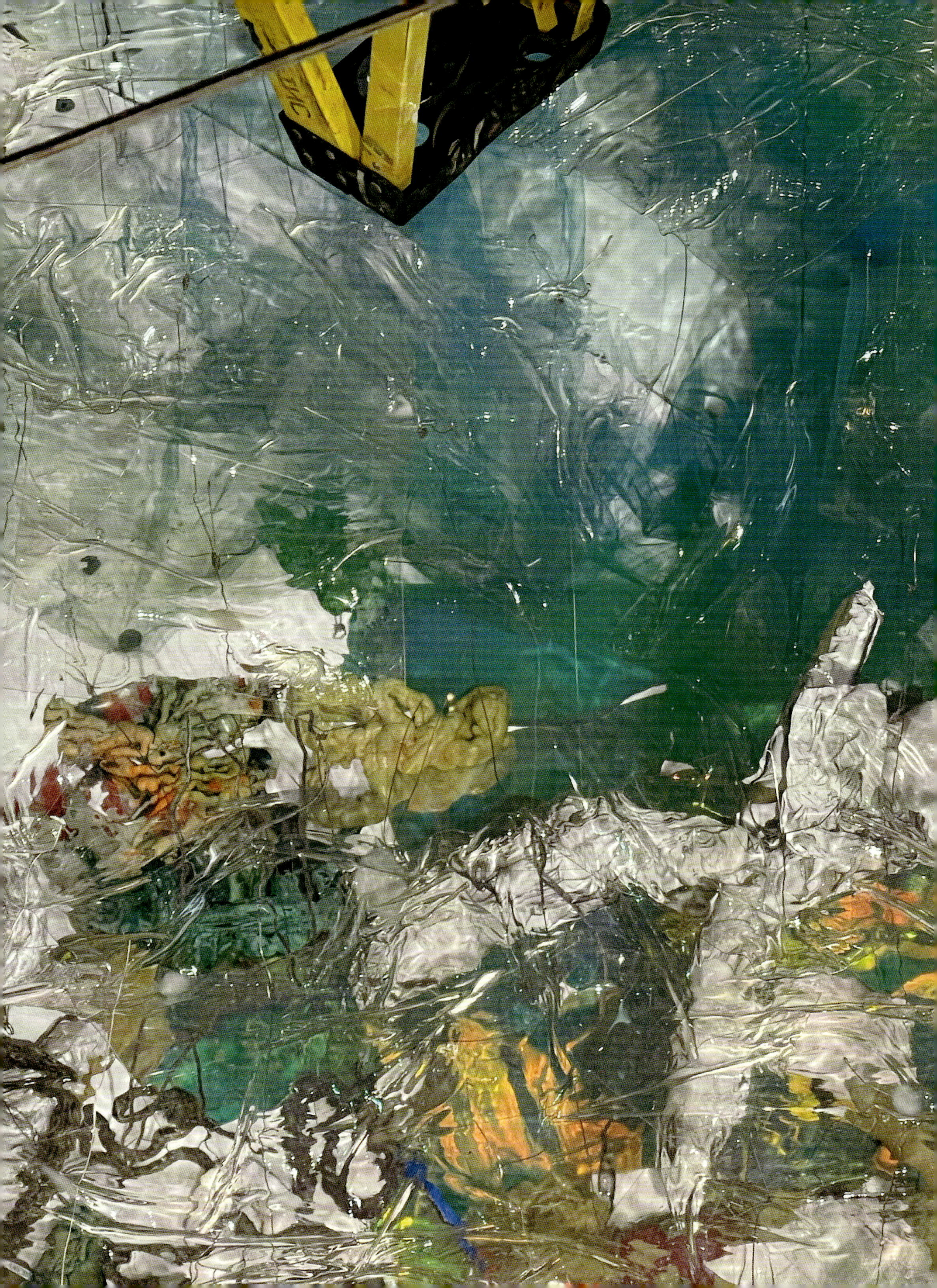

Making *if earth is the brain then where is the body*

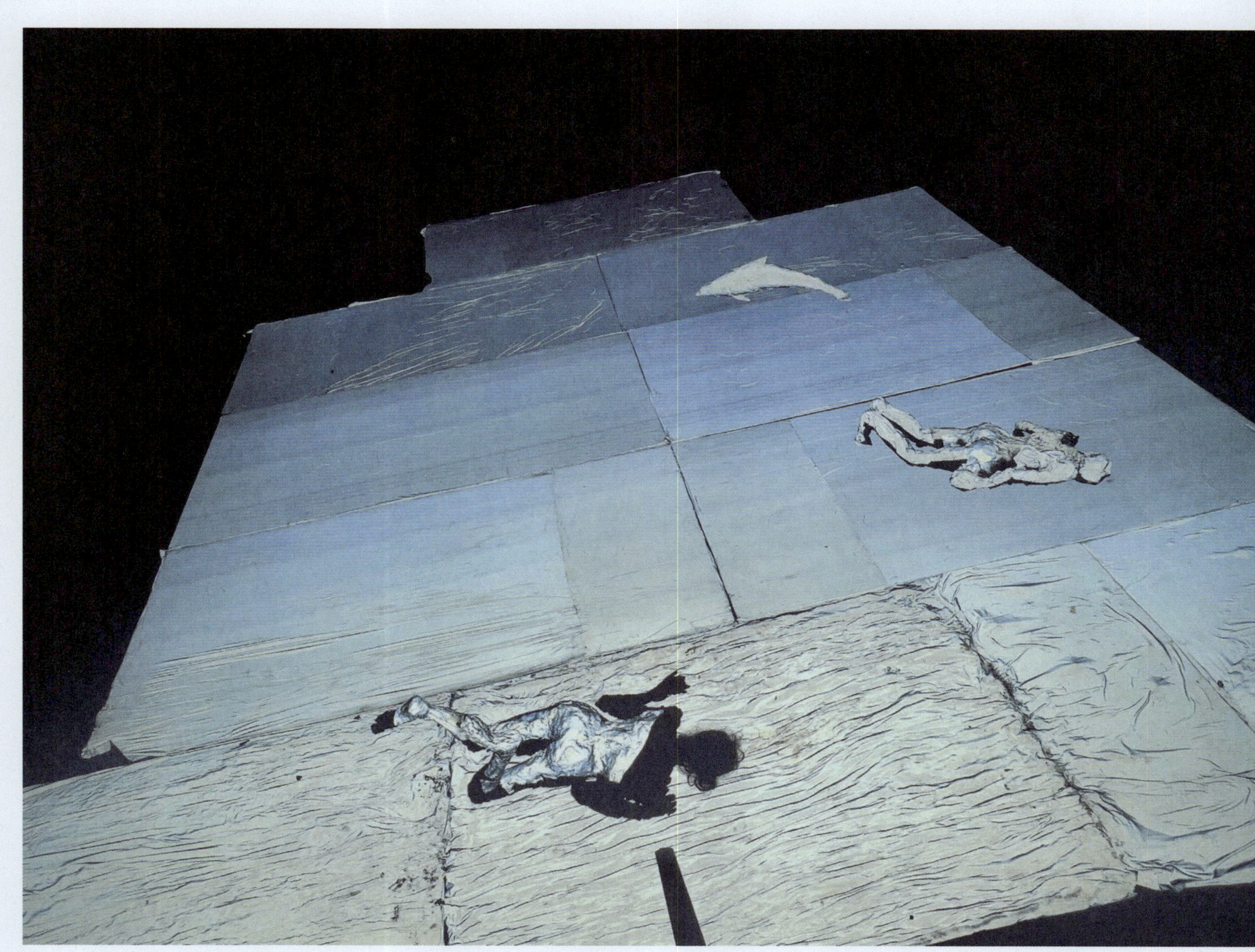

105

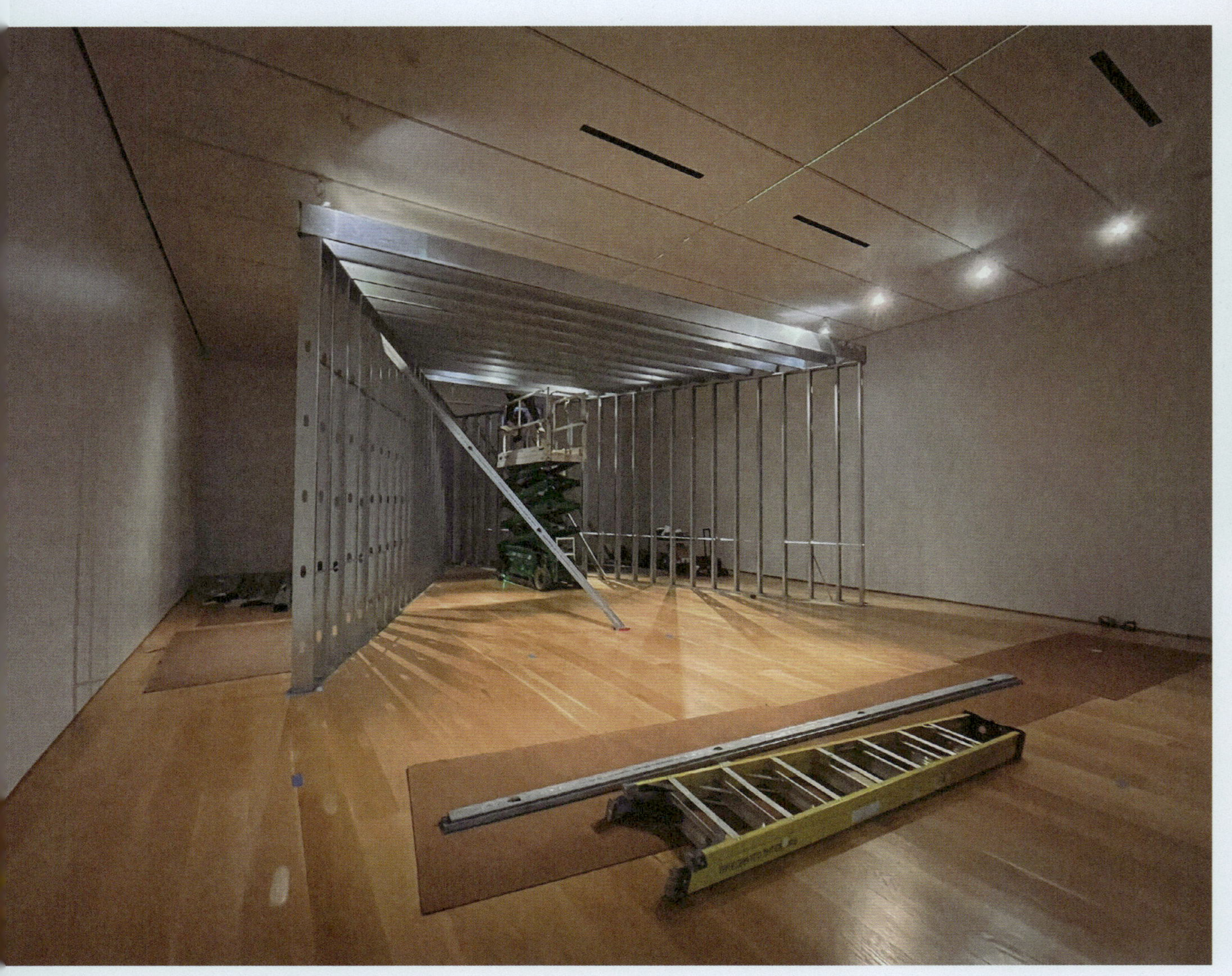

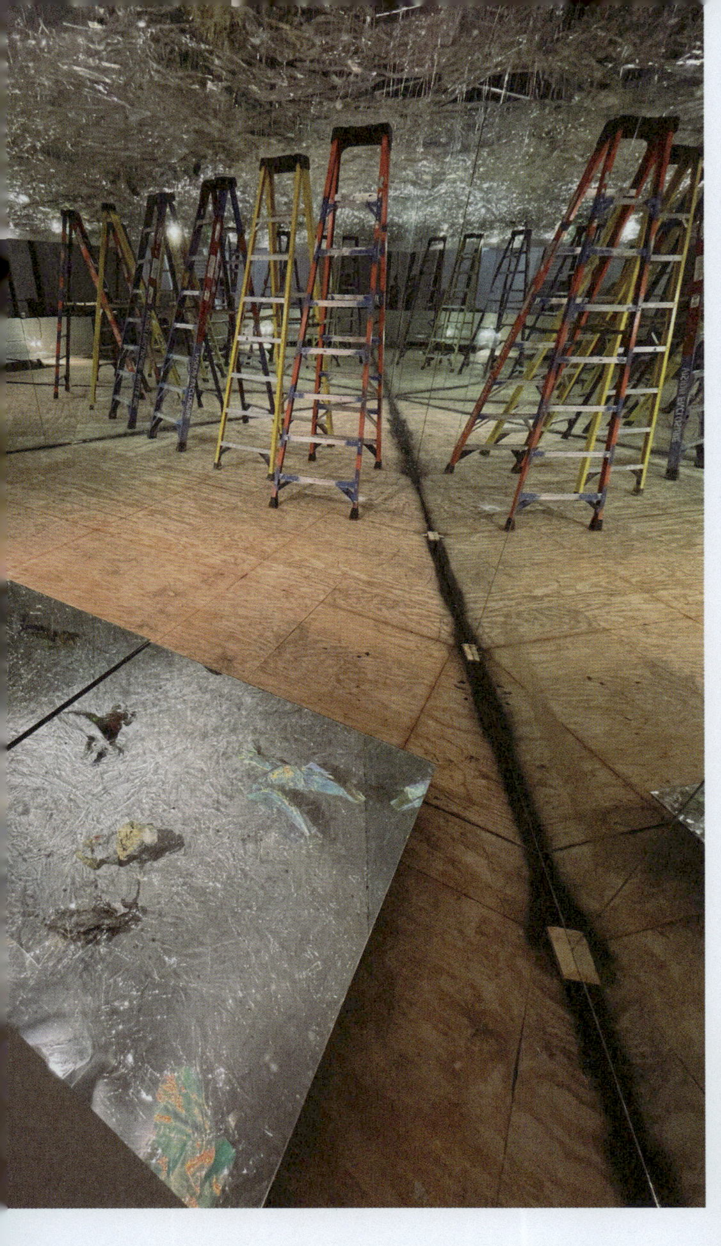

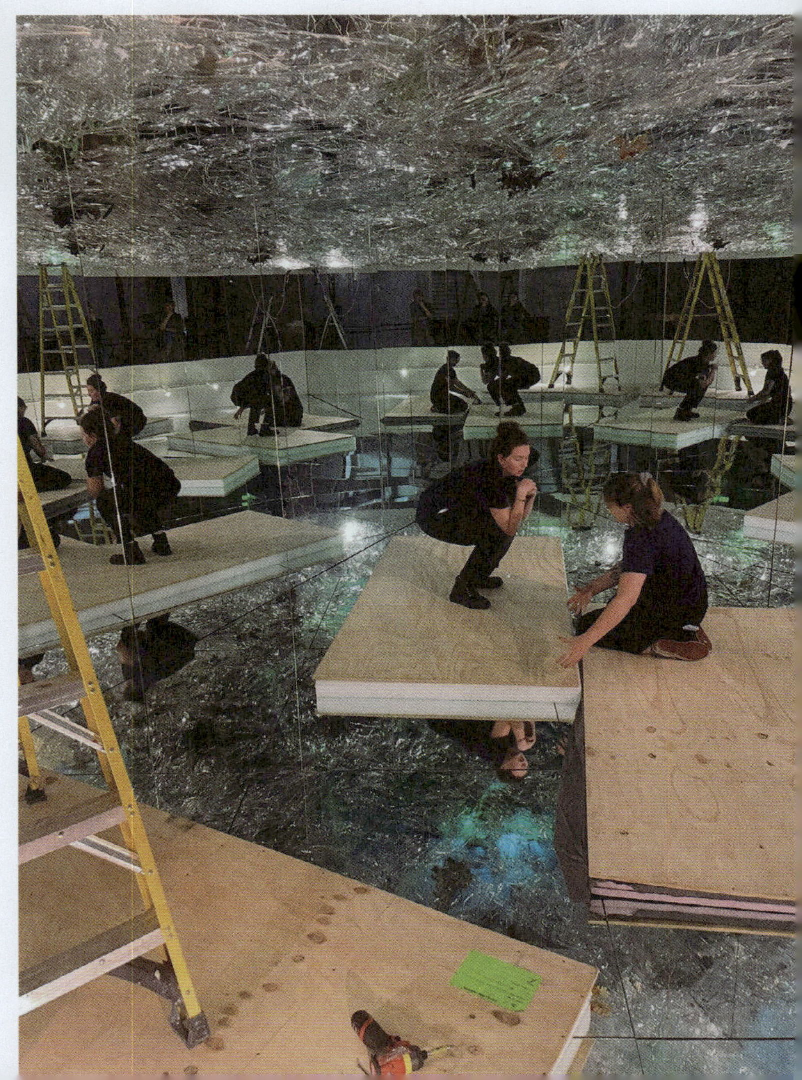

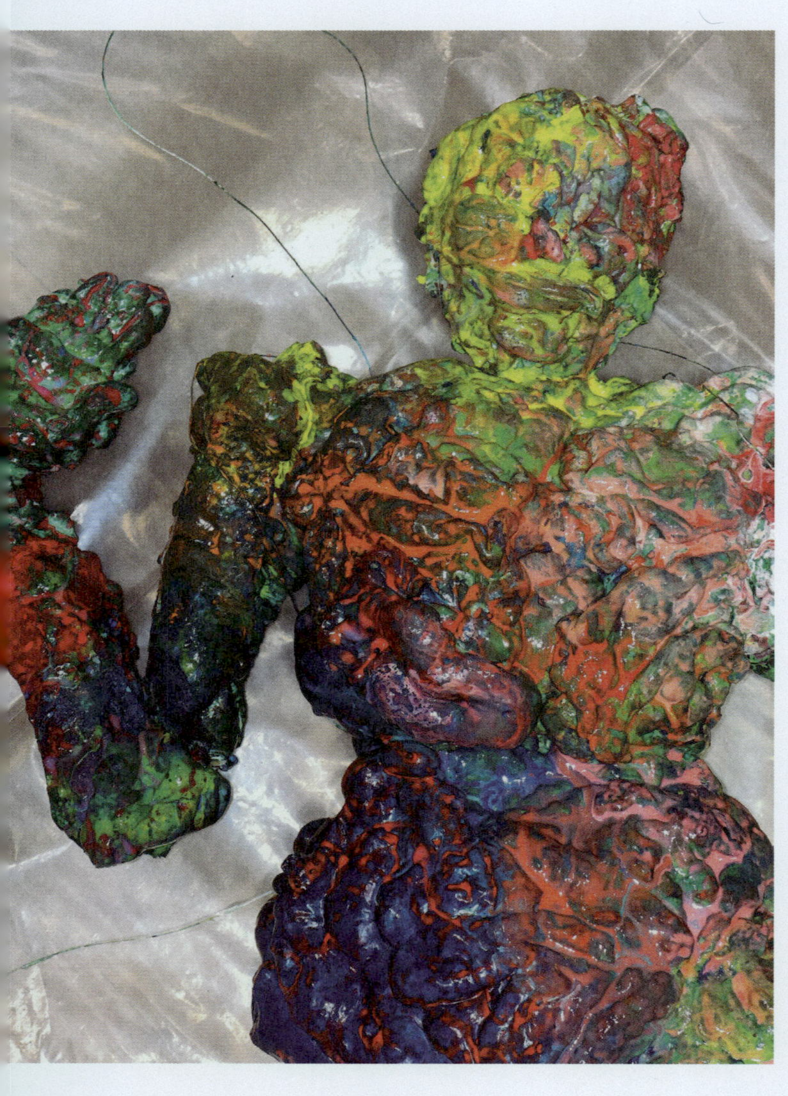
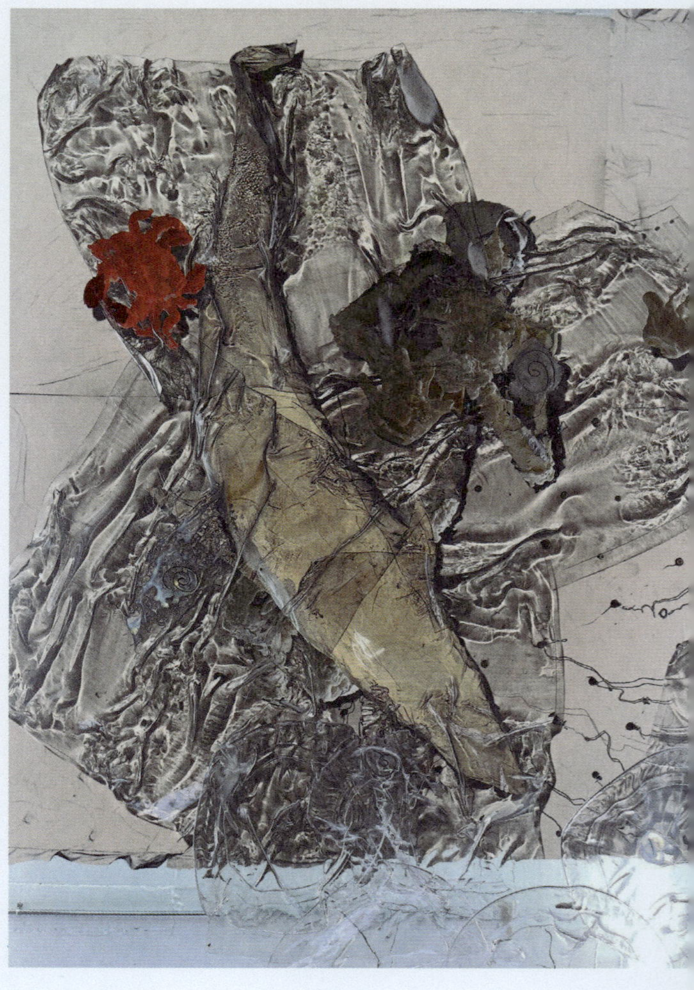

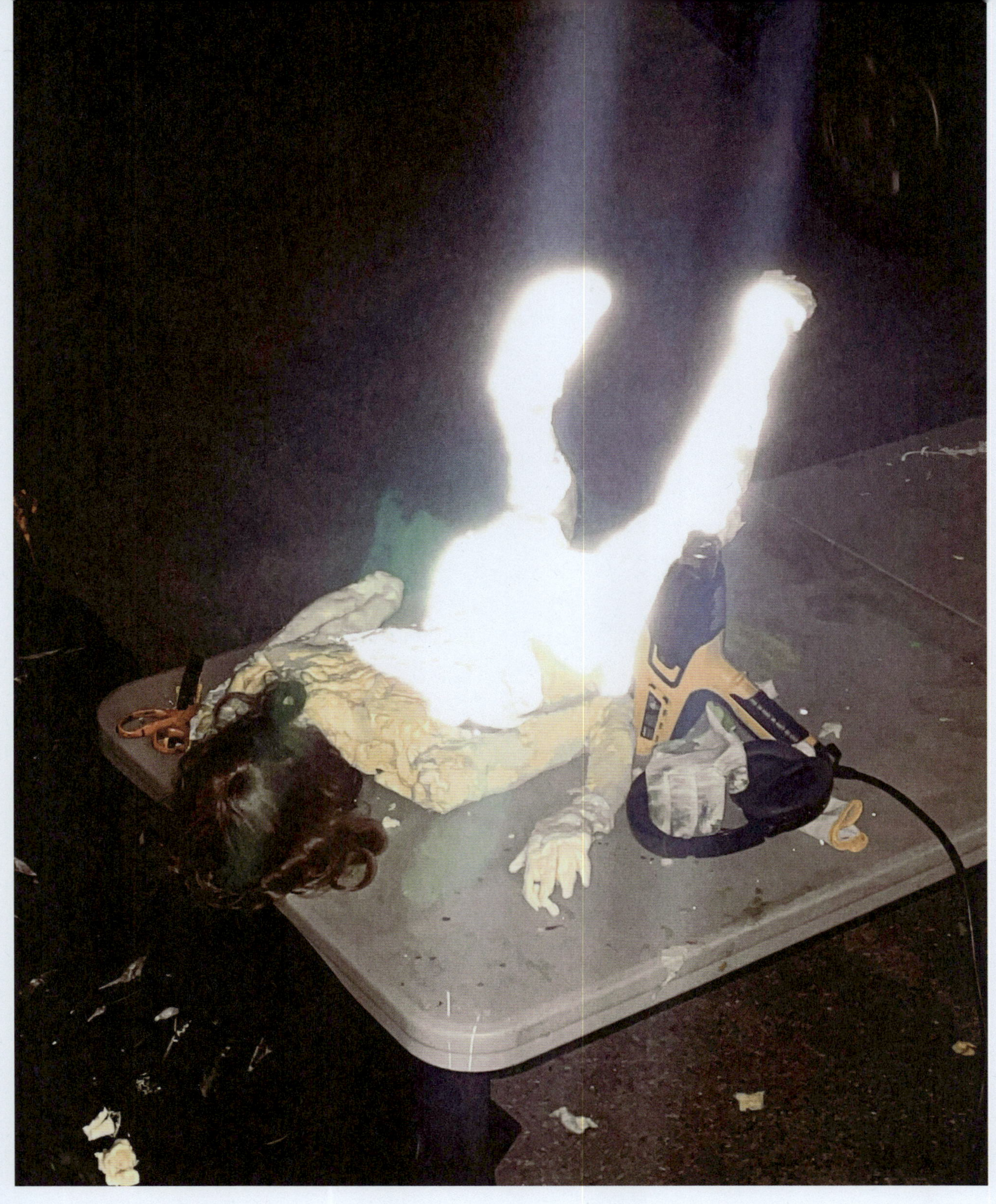

Born in Ann Arbor, Michigan, in 1973, Samara Golden lives and works in Los Angeles. After receiving a BFA at the Minneapolis College of Art and Design, she earned an MFA at Columbia University in New York in 2009, then relocated to Los Angeles. In addition to *if earth is the brain then where is the body* at the Nasher Sculpture Center, Dallas, she has had solo museum exhibitions at the Fabric Workshop and Museum, Philadelphia (2020); Yerba Buena Center for the Arts, San Diego (2016); and MoMA PS1, New York (2014). She has also exhibited large installations in group shows including *Dreamhome: Stories of Art and Shelter*, Art Gallery of New South Wales, Sydney, Australia (2022); *Psyche and Politics*, Staatliche Kunsthalle Baden-Baden, Germany (2019); the 2017 Whitney Biennial, Whitney Museum of American Art, New York; *Made in L.A. 2014*, Hammer Museum, Los Angeles (2014); and *Room to Live: Recent Acquisitions and Works from the Collection*, the Museum of Contemporary Art, Los Angeles (2013), among others.

Golden's works are held in the collections of the Art Gallery of New South Wales; Whitney Museum of American Art; Los Angeles County Museum of Art; Museum of Contemporary Art, Los Angeles; Orange County Museum of Art, Santa Ana; Zabludowicz Collection, London; and Yuz Collection, Shanghai. In 2015, a monograph on Golden was published by MoMA PS1, and her work has been written about in publications including *Artforum*, *Art in America*, *The New York Times*, *The New Yorker*, and *Mousse Magazine*.

Photography and Copyright Credits

All works of art unless otherwise specified are by Samara Golden.
© 2025 Samara Golden

All photographs of *Samara Golden: if earth is the brain then where is the body*
are by Samara Golden except those featured on pages 20–24, 33, 38–40,
70–71, 82–87, and 97–101: photographs by Kevin Todora, courtesy of Nasher
Sculpture Center

FIG. 1   Photograph by Kevin Todora, courtesy of Nasher Sculpture Center, Dallas
FIGS. 2–5, 8, 10–11   Courtesy of Samara Golden
FIG. 6   Photograph by Carlos Avendaño, courtesy of the Fabric Workshop and Museum
FIGS. 7, 9   Photographs by Nik Massey, courtesy of Night Gallery
FIGS. 12, 15, 16   Courtesy of Catherine Craft
FIG. 13   Courtesy of the Nasher Sculpture Center, Dallas
FIG. 14   Courtesy of iStockphoto.com/ferrantraite

Illustration Credits

FIG. 1   Nasher Sculpture Center, Dallas, 2016
FIG. 2   Installation view, Night Gallery, Los Angeles, 2011
FIG. 3   Installation view, Night Gallery, Los Angeles, 2014
FIG. 4   Installation view, MoMA PS1, New York, 2014
FIG. 5   Whitney Museum of American Art, New York; promised gift of Danielle Ryan.
           Installation view, 2017 Whitney Biennial, Whitney Museum of American Art, 2017
FIG. 6   Installation view, The Fabric Workshop and Museum, Philadelphia, 2020
FIG. 7   Installation view, Night Gallery, Los Angeles, 2022
FIG. 9   Installation view, Night Gallery, Los Angeles, 2022
FIG. 10   Installation view, *Psyche and Politics*, Staatliche Kunsthalle, Baden-Baden, 2019
FIG. 11   The Museum of Contemporary Art, Los Angeles; purchase with funds provided by
           the Curatorial Discretionary Fund. Installation view, *Room to Live: Recent Acquisitions
           and Works from the Collection*, The Museum of Contemporary Art, Los Angeles, 2013
FIG. 12   Musée Marmottan Monet, Paris; inv. 5163, legs. Michel Monet
FIG. 13   Raymond and Patsy Nasher Collection, Nasher Sculpture Center, Dallas

Samara Golden: if earth is the brain then where is the body is published on the occasion of the exhibition of the same name organized by the Nasher Sculpture Center, Dallas, Texas, September 28, 2024–January 12, 2025.

Samara Golden: if earth is the brain then where is the body is made possible by leading support from Frost Bank. Additional support is provided by the Dallas Art Fair Foundation, Dallas Tourism Public Improvement District (DTPID), Miyoung Lee, Karen Hillenburg, Carole Server, and Irwin N. Gold Family Foundation.

ISBN: 978-1-63681-217-5

Published in 2025 by the Nasher Sculpture Center and DelMonico Books • D.A.P.

Nasher Sculpture Center
2001 Flora Street
Dallas, Texas 75201
nashersculpturecenter.org

DelMonico Books
Available through ARTBOOK / D.A.P.
75 Broad Street, Suite 630
New York, NY 10004
artbook.com
delmonicobooks.com

Designed by Lorraine Wild and Xiaoqing Wang, Green Dragon Office, Los Angeles
Copyedited by Jane Hyun
Color separations by Echelon, Los Angeles
Printing by Lösch GmbH & Co. KG, Germany

ARTIST ACKNOWLEDGMENTS

Special thanks to John Seal, Fred Golden, Sue Golden, Alisa Golden, Davida Nemeroff and Night Gallery, Phil Grauer and Sarah Bramen and Canada Gallery, and especially Catherine Craft, for her belief in me and for the hours and hours of work that went into realizing this project and book with me.